Bilingual
Guide
to Japan

NINJA

KUROI Hiromitsu

Translated by Chris Glenn
Illustrated by IWASAKI Jun

SHOGAKUKAN

Bilingual Guide to Japan
NINJA

KUROI Hiromitsu
Illustrated by IWASAKI Jun

Book and Cover design © Kindaichi Design
English Translation © Chris Glenn

Published by
SHOGAKUKAN
2-3-1 Hitotsubashi Chiyoda-Ku,
Tokyo 101-8001 JAPAN
https://www.shogakukan.co.jp
https://japanesebooks.jp/en/

All rights reserved.
No part of this publication may be reproduced in any form or by any means, graphic, electronic or mechanical, including photocopying and recording by an information storage and retrieval system, without written permission from the publisher.

NINJA BILINGUAL GUIDE by
KUROI Hiromitsu, IWASAKI Jun, Chris Glenn
© 2019 KUROI Hiromitsu, IWASAKI Jun,
Chris Glenn, UCHIDA Kazuhiro / SHOGAKUKAN
Printed in Japan
ISBN 978-4-09-388728-1

忍者バイリンガルガイド

黒井宏光 監修
クリス グレン 訳
岩崎 隼 画

小学館

English Renderings of Ninja Terms

This English and Japanese bilingual book introduces the basic knowledge of Ninja.

All Japanese terms are rendered in Italicized Roman characters. The only diacritical mark used is the hyphen (-), to separate two adjacent vowel sounds.

Since the conventions for rendering these terms into English differ depending on the facility, terms used elsewhere may not be consistent with those used in this book. Given that even Japanese names and pronunciations may differ depending on the sect or region, they cannot be generalized. Standard names are used in this book and are rendered so that they can be easily read by individuals who are not native speakers of Japanese.

本書の英文表記について

この本は、忍者の基本的な知識について紹介しています。日本語が母語ではない人のために、英語で訳してあります。

日本語はすべてローマ字読みにし、斜体のアルファベットで表記しています。発音は、母音が続いてしまう場合のみハイフン（-）を使用しています。

※これら外国語表記は、施設（公共施設、地方自治体等）ごとに異なるルールで表記されているため、本書と一致しない場合があります。地方によって日本語でも呼び方が異なることがあり、一般化はできません。本書では標準的な呼称を掲載し、外国語を母語とする読者ができるだけ平易に発音できる表記としました。

Table of Contents 目次

Introduction 6　　はじめに

Chapter 1　　第一章
History of the Ninja　　忍者の歴史

Appearance of the Ninja 12　　忍者の登場
The Age of Ninja Activity 13　　忍者の活躍の時代
Ninja and Shogunate 14　　忍者と将軍
The End of the Ninja Era 15　　忍者の時代の終焉
Iga and Koka 16　　伊賀と甲賀
Ninja Disciplines 18　　忍者の流派
Ninja and Castles 20　　忍者と城

Chapter 2　　第二章
Learning Ninjutsu　　忍術を学ぶ

Ninjutsu Densho 24　Ninja no Okite 26　　忍術伝書　忍者の掟
Breathing Methods 28　Walking Methods 30　　呼吸法　歩き方
Running Methods 32　　走り方
Jumping and Landing Methods 34　　跳び方と降り方
Fire Handling Methods 36　　火の利用法
Searching for Drinking Water 38　　飲み水の探し方
Determining Directions 40　Determining the Weather 42　　方位を知る　天気を知る
Determining the Time 44　Yaei-jutsu 46　　時刻を知る　野営術
Shinnyu-jutsu 48　Ongyo-jutsu 50　　侵入術　隠形術
Intoku-jutsu 52　Touso-jutsu 54　　隠匿術　逃走術
Henso-jutsu/Disguise Techniques 56　　変装術
Appearance Changing Techniques 58　　変相術
Joho Dentatsu-jutsu 60　Ango-jutsu 62　　情報伝達術　暗号術
Kioku-jutsu 64　Taijin-jutsu 66　　記憶術　対人術
Seishin Toitsu-jutsu 68　Kunoichi-no-jutsu 70　　精神統一術　くノ一の術
Secrets of the Ninja House 72　　忍者屋敷の秘密

Chapter 3　　第三章
Ninja Tools　　忍者の道具

Shinobi Shozoku 78　Shinobi Roku-gu 80　　忍び装束　忍び六具
Shuriken 82　Katana 84　　手裏剣　刀
Giso Buki 86　Kama and Kasugai 88　　擬装武器　鎌とかすがい
Tekkokagi, Tekken and Kakute 90　　手甲鉤、鉄拳、角手
Fukiya and Fukumibari 92　Kaki 94　Suiki 96　　吹き矢とふくみ針　火器　水器
Toki 98　Ninja Rations 100　　登器　忍者の食事

Appendix　　付録
Glossary 104　　用語集
Ninja Villages to Visit　　訪ねてみたい忍者の里

Ninja Museum of Iga-ryu 118　　伊賀流忍者博物館
Koka Ninja House 122　　甲賀流忍術屋敷

Introduction: What Are the Ninja?

Origins of the Ninja

During the 7th century Asuka period an esoteric sect of Buddhism called *Shugendo* was founded by En no Ozunu. The ascetic practitioners of *Shugendo* ran around in the mountains, climbing rocks and acquiring extraordinary abilities, which led to them being feared by the local villagers. The theory is that En no Ozunu and his followers formed the basic roots of the ninja.

According to old records, the Asuka period prince, regent and statesman, Shotoku Taishi, was assisted in a spy-like capacity by one Otomono Sainyu, a *shinobi* (p. 104) who sought and provided information to the prince. In the 15th and 16th century Sengoku period (p. 104), when ninja were most active, various warlords from across the country employed ninja in an effort to obtain information regarding their enemies. The start of the peaceful years of the Edo period (p. 105) meant, however, that the scope for ninja's activity considerably reduced.

はじめに──忍者とは何か
●忍者の起源
　7世紀の飛鳥時代、役小角という人物によって修験道という宗教が誕生した。修験道の行者たちは山を駆け回り、そそり立つ岩をよじ登り、人並みはずれた能力を身につけ、里に暮らす人々から恐れられた。この役小角をはじめとする修験道の行者たちが忍者のルーツであるという説がある。
　古い記録では、飛鳥時代の大伴細入という人物は「志能便」として政治家の聖徳太子に仕えたといい、聖徳太子に情報を提供する忍者であったと考えられる（忍び　p.104）。日本史の中で忍者がもっとも活躍した時代が15〜16世紀の戦国時代（p.104）で、全国各地の武将たちは敵の情報を得るためにさかんに忍者をやとった。平和な江戸時代（p.105）になると、忍者の活躍の場は少なくなった。

What Is *Ninjutsu*?

The most important task for a ninja is to gather intelligence information on the enemy and report it to their employer. Various ninja techniques and skills, known collectively as *ninjutsu,* are used to accomplish these missions. Depending on the situation, any number of skills could be called upon, such as infiltrating mansions, walking stealthily, stealing things, and making quick getaways. *Ninjutsu* developed greatly during the Sengoku period, when ninja played an increasingly active role.

This book explains the ninja arts, tools, and weapons of *ninjutsu*, and introduces the daily mind and body training methods used by the ninja.

In addition, the ninja had a wealth of skills, such as predicting the weather, telling the time, making medicine from herbs, and were skilled in various survival techniques. The wisdom of the ninja can also be useful for people in the modern age.

●忍術とは

忍者のもっとも重要な仕事は敵の情報を探り、それを雇い主に報告することである。その任務遂行のためにさまざまな忍術を用いる。屋敷に忍び込んで、音を立てずに歩いて物を盗み、いかにすばやく立ち去るかなど、状況に応じてさまざまな術が用いられる。忍術は忍者の活躍の場が増えた戦国時代に大きく発展した。

本書では、さまざまな忍術、忍具と呼ばれる道具や武器を解説するとともに、それらを用いるために忍者が日々行っていた心身の鍛錬法についても紹介する。

また、忍者は天気を予測したり、時刻を知ったり、薬草から薬を作るなどの知識を豊富に持っており、現代でいうサバイバル術に長けていた。これら忍者の知恵は現代人にも役立つことが多いはずだ。

The Real Ninja

Many popular ninja novels, ninja movies, ninja comics, and entertainments have been created in Japan, and have captured the hearts of many people, especially children. Not just the Japanese, but people around the world are fascinated by ninja, with the word "NINJA" now being universally recognized. Many international tourists visit ninja related sites, such as Iga-ueno in Mie Prefecture, while others come to Japan to practice *ninjutsu*.

Needless to say, ninja are not fantasy heroes. They were highly active agents who acquired extraordinary abilities and skills through repeated, dedicated training. Knowing specifically what ninja did, how they lived and how they trained will help us to better understand the true image of the ninja.

●忍者の本当の姿

　日本ではこれまでに数々の忍者小説、忍者映画、忍者漫画などが作られ、子どもたちをはじめとして多くの人の心をとらえてきた。忍者に心を奪われたのは日本人ばかりではなく、いまや「NINJA」は世界に通用する言葉となっている。多くの外国人が三重県伊賀市をはじめとした忍者ゆかりの地を訪問し、わざわざ海外から日本へ忍者修行に来る人も少なくない。

　いうまでもなく、忍者は空想上のヒーローではない。かつて実際に活躍した人たちであり、厳しい修行を重ねることで人並みはずれた能力を身につけた人たちである。忍者がどんな仕事をし、どのように暮らし、どのように修行を積んだかを具体的に知ることが、忍者の実像の理解につながるだろう。

Chapter 1

History of the Ninja

第一章

忍者の歴史

Appearance of the Ninja
Ancient Times to the Kamakura Period (1185-1333)

The history of *ninjutsu* dates back so far, it is not clear when or how it was formed. According to one theory, ancient Chinese martial arts and sorcery techniques were introduced to Japan and evolved into *ninjutsu*.

Ninjutsu is closely related to Japan's *Shugendo*, esoteric Buddhism doctrines, whereby *yamabushi* (mountain ascetics) would undergo extensive training in the mountains to develop extraordinary physical abilities and mystical powers. By subjecting themselves to this rigorous existence in nature, they gained a wide range of life experiences and survival knowledge. Much of what has been transmitted from *ninjutsu* remains relevant to this day.

In the ancient Asuka period (593-710), the politically active Prince Shotoku (574-622) and Emperor Tenmu (?-686) are said to have used ninja. During the late 12th century, the rival warrior clans, the Genji and the Heishi are believed to have fought with ninja in their ranks.

忍者の登場 古代～鎌倉時代 (1185～1333)

忍術の歴史はとても古く、いつどのように生まれたのかはっきりしない。一説には古代の中国で用いられた兵法や占術などが日本に伝わり、忍術にとり込まれたともいわれる。

忍術は日本の修験道とも深い関わりがある。山伏（修験道の修行者）は険しい山の中で修行することで人並みはずれた身体能力や呪術を身につけた。また、自然の中で暮らすことで、生きるためのさまざまな知恵や知識を得た。これらはいまに伝えられる忍術と共通するものがたくさんある。

日本の飛鳥時代 (593～710) では聖徳太子 (574～622) や天武天皇 (?～686) が忍者を使ったともいわれる。また、12世紀後半の源氏と平氏（ともに武士を代表する一族）は、たがいに忍者を使って戦ったといわれる。

The Age of Ninja Activity
The Sengoku Period (1467-1615)

Ninja were most active during the Sengoku, or Warring States period. The various *daimyo* (p. 106), powerful warlords, emerged across Japan fighting one another in their efforts to expand their territories and power bases. Because of their extraordinary physical abilities and powers, ninja were employed to infiltrate enemy territory, and report back on the political situation, troop numbers and weaponry. Due to such intelligence gathering, the warlords would gain an advantage over the enemy.

On the onset of battle, the ninja's role was to advance forward, gather intelligence on the enemy's situation, and to launch surprise attacks. Ninja possessed great knowledge of gunpowder, and so they were often active in the artillery corps. They would also infiltrate enemy positions and spread false information to confuse and confound the enemy.

忍者の活躍の時代　戦国時代（1467〜1615）

　忍者がもっとも活躍したのは戦国時代だ。日本各地に大名（p.106）という力のある領主が現れて、自分の領土を広げようと争いあった。戦国大名たちは、忍者の人並みはずれた身体能力や情報収集力を活用して、敵を倒そうとした。ふだんから忍者を敵国に潜入させて、領主がどんな政治を行っているか、兵力や武器をどれくらい持っているかなどを探らせた。敵の情報をあらかじめ知ることで優位に立てるからだ。

　合戦の際に、先回りして敵の様子をうかがったり、奇襲攻撃をしかけたりするのは忍者の仕事だった。忍者は火薬の知識が豊富なので、鉄砲隊としても活躍した。また、敵陣に忍び込んで、嘘の情報を流して敵を混乱させることもした。

Ninja and Shogunate
The Edo Period (1603-1868)

Tokugawa Ieyasu (1542-1616, p. 107) was the warlord who established the Edo *Bakufu* (p. 108). Ieyasu recognized the abilities and the value of the ninja, having personally experienced assistance by the ninja of Koka and Iga when escaping from pursuing enemies. When he became the ruler of Japan, he employed many ninja.

The elite ninja who served the shogunate directly were known as *Iga-gumi Doushin*. They relocated to Edo (modern-day Tokyo) and worked as bodyguards, security and as artillery riflemen. The 8th Shogun, Tokugawa Yoshimune (1684-1751, p. 109) was originally the lord of Kishu, modern-day Wakayama prefecture, and when he was made Shogun, he relocated to Edo, but took along ninja from his province, making them his personal elite ninja. They were known as *Oniwaban* (p. 110) and gathered information under the direction of Yoshimune, and maintained surveillance on various warlords and persons of interest.

忍者と将軍　江戸時代（1603～1868）

　徳川家康（1542～1616、p.107）は、江戸幕府（p.108）を開いた武将だ。家康は敵に追われたときに甲賀忍者と伊賀忍者に助けられた経験から、忍者の能力を認めるようになる。幕府を開いて天下を治めるようになると多くの忍者を召し抱えた。

　幕府に仕えた伊賀の忍者には、「伊賀組同心」と呼ばれる者たちがいる。彼らは江戸（現在の東京）に住んで、警備やボディガードなどの仕事や鉄砲を使う仕事についた。江戸幕府8代将軍の徳川吉宗（1684～1751、p.109）は、もとは紀州藩（和歌山県を中心に治めた藩）の藩主だったが、将軍に就任して江戸に向かうときに紀州の忍者を一緒に連れてきて、自分専用の忍者にした。彼らは「御庭番」（p.110）と呼ばれ、吉宗の指示で情報を集めたり、要注意人物や大名を監視したりした。

The End of the Ninja Era

Following the Warring States period when battles ceased, and during the peaceful years of the Edo period, the ninja were entrusted with reconnaissance and security work. The Edo Shogunate had placed Japan in a self-imposed exile, prohibiting communications and exchange with foreign countries. Despite this, in 1853 an American fleet led by Commodore Matthew Perry in a coal-fired steam frigate known to the Japanese as a *kurofune,* or black ship, arrived at Uraga (Yokosuka, Kanagawa prefecture), and demanded trade with Japan. At this time, a ninja was sent on a mission to board and search the foreign vessels.

With the collapse of the shogunate in 1868, and the beginning of Japan's Meiji restoration, the role of the ninja, along with the shogunate and the *daimyo* they served, also came to an end. To survive, the ninja turned to occupations that used their knowledge and expertise, such as agriculture, police officers, fireworks specialists or doctors.

Although there are presently no professional ninja, *ninjutsu* has been inherited by a few who train in the discipline and work to preserve the skills and wonders of the ninja.

忍者の時代の終焉

合戦のなくなった江戸時代、忍者はおもに偵察の仕事をまかされて、世の中の治安を陰で守った。江戸幕府は外国との交流を禁じていたが、1853年にマシュー・ペリーが率いるアメリカ艦隊(「黒船」)が浦賀(神奈川県横須賀市)に来航して日本との貿易などを要求した。このとき、使節団の一員として忍者が黒船を探った。

1868年に幕府がなくなり、明治時代が始まると、幕府や各地の大名に仕えていた忍者もその役目を終える。忍者たちは農家、警察官、花火師、医者など、自分たちの知識や経験の活きる仕事を選択して生活していった。

そして現在、忍者を仕事とする人はいないが、自分の鍛錬のために修行する人や、忍者の魅力を伝えるために活動する人たちによって忍術は受け継がれている。

Iga and Koka

The two famous ninja regions are Iga and Koka. Iga is located in Mie prefecture's western districts, while Koka is in the southern areas of Shiga prefecture.

Both regions thrived as major centers of esoteric Buddhism, and the knowledge and abilities of the *yamabushi* were adopted by the ninja of Iga and Koka. The people of these regions did not consider *ninjutsu* to be out of the ordinary, as they had become accustomed to the arts during the long periods of civil war.

Sengoku period Iga and Koka ninja have become world renown for their exceptional abilities. Because there were no ruling lords in the Iga and Koka regions and therefore no affiliations, various warlords attempted to engage their services. Both areas are close to the old capital, Kyoto, and so there was ample opportunity to play an active part in the political scene there, making them famous.

伊賀と甲賀

忍者の里として有名なのが伊賀と甲賀のふたつの地域だ。伊賀は、現在の三重県西部に位置し、甲賀は現在の滋賀県南部に位置する。

伊賀と甲賀は古くから修験道がさかんな地で、山伏たちが身につけた知恵や能力が伊賀や甲賀の忍術に関係しているといわれる。伊賀と甲賀の人々にとって、忍術とは自分たちが受け継いできた戦乱の時代に生きる知恵の集大成であって、けっして特別なものではなかった。

　伊賀と甲賀の忍者は、戦国時代になるとその能力の高さが世に知られるようになる。伊賀と甲賀には有力な領主がいなかったので、日本各地の領主にやとわれることができた。2つの地域は政治の中心の京都に近く、活躍する機会が多かったのが有名になった理由だ。

Ninja Disciplines

The majority of ninja active during the Sengoku period hailed from Iga or Koka. Various Sengoku *daimyo* employed the Iga and Koka ninja in a number of roles, mostly that of information gathering and participating in battles. Some of these ninja remained in their areas of employment long after the Sengoku and Edo period, organizing their own *ryuha*, groups with a unique set of techniques and ideas.

Iga-ueno Castle (Iga, Mie)
伊賀上野城（三重県伊賀市）

忍者の流派

　忍者がもっとも活躍した戦国時代には、忍者のほとんどは伊賀か甲賀の出身だったともいわれている。伊賀・甲賀の忍者たちは各地の戦国大名にやとわれて、情報を集めたり、合戦に参加したりするなど、さまざまな仕事をした。それらの忍者のうち、戦国時代が終わって江戸時代になっても各地に残って忍者として活躍し、独自の流派（独特の技術や考え方を持っている集団）を名乗る者もいた。

For example, the *Nusumi-gumi*, a band of ninja serving the Kaga domain of modern-day Ishikawa prefecture during the Edo period were originally from Iga. Ninja were called many different things in different parts of the country, and the word "ninja" wasn't actually used until the Taisho period (1912-1926).

Kanazawa Castle (Kanazawa, Ishikawa)
金沢城（石川県金沢市）

たとえば、江戸時代に加賀藩（現在の石川県）に仕えた忍者集団「ぬすみ組」はもともと伊賀出身の忍者だった。忍者の呼び方は各地さまざまで、「忍者」という言葉が一般に使われるようになったのは大正時代（1912～1926）になってからだ。

Ninja and Castles

Castles where warlords lived were surrounded by moats, stone and earthen walls to prevent intruders. Some of the impressive, sloping stone walls featured a sudden incline called a *musha-gaeshi* (lit. warrior turn-back), to prevent the scaling of the walls (1). At the top of these walls and around the base of the watchtowers were rows of skewer-like spikes called *shinobi-gaeshi* (2), or ninja turn-backs, while another mechanism known as an *ishi-otoshi* (3), or stone dropping chute, was intended to shoot matchlock guns on downward angles for greater defensive power.

1

忍者と城

　大名が住む城のまわりには堀がめぐらされ、石垣や土塁が築かれていて侵入者を阻む。石垣の中には、上に登っていくにしたがって勾配が急になってゆく「武者返し」(1)という積み方をしているものもある。また石垣の上に建つ櫓には、「忍び返し」(2)と呼ばれる、尖った串状のものが取り付けられていたり、「石落とし」(3)と呼ばれる、壁から張り出した開口部から鉄砲を撃ちかけるしかけもあったりする。

Even if you were able to penetrate the stone and earthen walls, there were a variety of defensive devices to prevent you from reaching the castle's main central *honmaru* baily. Paths and routes within the castle grounds twist and turn in a maze-like fashion, overlooked by walls featuring *sama*, arrow slits and gun ports. There are hidden rooms and hallways with creaking floors to signal intruder alert.

　石垣や土塁を越えて城の中に侵入できたとしても、城の中心に位置する「本丸」にたどり着くまでには、さまざまなしかけが待ち受けている。城内の道が折れ曲がっていて迷路のようになっていたり、「狭間」という壁に開けられた穴から鉄砲や矢を放たれたりすることもある。建物の内部も、歩くと音が鳴る廊下や隠し部屋などがある。

Chapter 2

Learning Ninjustu

第二章

忍術を学ぶ

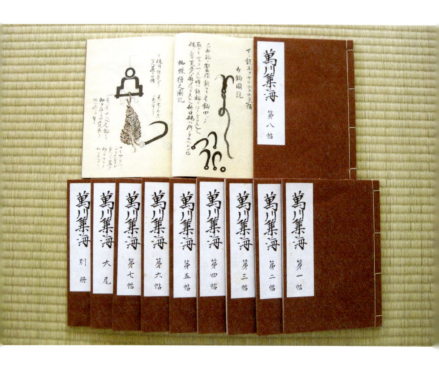

Ninjutsu Densho
(Ninjustu Texts)

The various techniques used by ninja are called *ninjutsu*. *Ninjutsu* was originally handed down verbally from parents to children and from masters to apprentices in a system called *kuden*. If the arts of *ninjutsu* were recorded on paper, they may have fallen into the hands of the enemy, likewise, students learned from their masters by repeating their actions, something that can't be studied from reading a book.

However, when the ninja's most active Warring States period ended, and the peaceful Edo period began, the need for ninja decreased, and it was feared that *ninjutsu* would be forgotten. For this reason *ninjutsu densho*, books summarizing *ninjutsu*, started to be written (left page).

Most of the *ninjutsu densho* were written in the Edo period. However, they fail to record all the details, and are written in a way that only practitioners of *ninjutsu* would understand.

忍術伝書

忍者が使ったさまざまな術を「忍術」という。忍術は親から子へ、師匠から弟子へと語り継がれていくものだった(「口伝」という)。忍術を紙に書いておくと敵に渡ってしまう可能性もあるし、実際に師匠が術をやって見せたり、弟子がそれをまねしたりしながらでないとわからないことが多いのが理由だ。

しかし、忍者が活躍した戦国時代が終わり、平和な江戸時代になって忍者の出番が少なくなると、忍術が忘れられていく恐れが出てきた。そのため、忍術をまとめた本である「忍術伝書」(左ページ)が書かれるようになった。

忍術伝書の多くは江戸時代に書かれたものだ。ただし、忍術伝書にも、かんじんな部分は書かれていなかったり、忍術を習った者にしかわからないように書いてあったりするものもある。

Ninja no Okite
(Ninja Law)

For ninja, the most important bond is the spirit, known as *seishin*. The ninja had a strong sense of righteousness believing that *ninjutsu* should never be used for personal gain. An oath to this effect was sworn before learning *ninjutsu*. Ninja would have to infiltrate people's homes, steal things, and sometimes even kill people. Seen from modern sensibilities, this is wrong. However, during the Warring States period in which the ninja lived, it was a means to survive, and they undertook such work believing it was best for the province they served.

The ninja were forbidden from doing many things including drinking, becoming close to women, or being greedy, desiring riches and possessions, and so such things were strictly controlled. Revealing gunpowder manufacturing techniques and other secret ninja tactics was also strictly forbidden.

忍者の掟

忍者にとって、もっとも大事な掟は「正心」といわれる心構えだ。正心とは「忍術は正しいと信じることのみに使い、けっして自分の利益のために使ってはならない」ということ。この心構えは忍術を習う前に必ず誓わされた。忍者は人の家に忍び込み、物を盗み、ときには人を殺す。現代の感覚から見れば悪いことばかりである。しかし、忍者が生きた戦国時代は、自分が仕える国のために正しいと信じることを行うことが生き抜くための手段だった。

忍者には禁止されていたことが多く、なかでも「酒、色（女性に心を乱すこと）、欲（金や物に心を奪われること）」は厳しく禁止されていた。また火薬の製法や秘密の術は絶対にもらしてはいけなかった。

Breathing Methods

For the ninja, something considered even more frightening than facing an enemy were the *shinobi-no-sanbyo* (lit. three ailments of the shinobi). The three ailments are: fearing the enemy more than necessary, underestimating the enemy, and thinking too much before taking action. To overcome these afflictions, it was considered most important to adjust their breathing. Through proper breathing methods, the ninja could calm their mind, spirit and soul (1).

The ability to breathe silently was one of the ninja's representative techniques. First sit upright in the *seiza* position (on your knees with feet tucked under you) and breathe in through your nose, deep down to your stomach. Next, consciously feel the breath permeate your entire body. Then gently, slowly release it via the nose (2).

When uttering a *kiai* (lit. power shout) performed by martial artists, after adjusting your breathing and posture, clench your fists above your head, and let out a cry that emanates from below your navel. This is called *inyo-no-kiai*, or yin-yang cosmic dual forces convergence of energy.

呼吸法

忍者にとって敵よりも恐ろしいのは「忍びの三病」という心の乱れである。三病とは、敵を必要以上にこわがること、敵を軽く見ること、行動する前に考えすぎることだ。これら三病をしりぞけるには呼吸を整えることが第一。呼吸を整えることで体の中に「気」をみなぎらせて心を落ち着けるのだ (1)。

忍者の呼吸法の代表が「無息忍」という音を出さずに静かに呼吸する方法。まず正座して、細く長く鼻から腹へ息を吸い込んで止める。次に吸い込んだ息を全身にめぐらせるよう意識する。そして鼻から細く長く息を吐く。紙きれを水につけて鼻にはり、息でゆれたり落ちたりしないように練習する (2)。

気合いを入れるときには、呼吸と体勢を整えたのちに両手をこぶしに握って頭上にかまえ、掛け声とともにへその下あたりに打ち下ろす。これを「陰陽の気合」という。

Walking Methods

The ninja practiced diligently how to walk silently indoors. The main ways of walking silently are as follows.

Shinobi-ashi: a way of walking through darkened buildings with many stairs and obstacles. Raise the leg high and gently step, *nuki-ashi* (1), setting the little toe down softly first, *sashi-ashi* (2), then repeat. *Suri-ashi*: a way of walking slowly without raising your feet, or stumbling over obstacles as you cross the floor. *Shime-ashi*: a style of walking making it easy to avoid attacks. Walk so that the knees remain together as you shuffle forward. *Kizami-ashi*: a style of walking that makes it easier to suddenly draw the *katana* (p. 111). Keeping the right foot forward, and the body standing at an angle, slowly move forward. *Shinso-toho*: in a squatting posture, step on the back of your hands and walk. These styles were used when walking in rooms where people were sleeping in a way that makes the least noise, and prevented stumbling on obstacles.

歩き方

忍者は建物の中で音を立てずに歩く方法を徹底的に練習した。おもな歩き方は次のとおり。

忍び足:真っ暗な中、段差や物がたくさんある建物の中を静かに歩く方法。そっと抜くように高く足を上げる「抜き足」(1) と、上げた足を差し出すように前に小指から下ろす「差し足」(2) を繰り返す。すり足:段差などでつまずかないように、足を上げずに床をするようにゆっくり足を出して歩く。締め足:攻撃をかわしやすい歩き方。すり足の歩き方で内股にして膝がこすれるくらいにして歩く。刻み足:刀 (p.111) を抜きやすいように、右足を前にして足も体も斜め向きで少しずつ進む。深草兎歩:しゃがんだ姿勢で手の甲に足をのせて歩く。もっとも音を立てず、物につまずかない歩き方で、人が寝ている部屋などを歩くときに使う。

Running Methods

Ninja were also known as *hayamichi-no-mono* (lit. shortcut people). Ninja often had to run quickly to convey the information obtained, but unlike the modern sense of running, it should be considered a method of walking quickly.

When you run, you don't look to the distance, but down to an area close around you. The reason being that if your jaw is raised, your breathing flow is interrupted and you will tire easily. The secret to the Iga ninja's running method is a breathing technique known as *futae-ibuki* (lit. double breath). The act involves repeatedly inhaling, exhaling, exhaling, then inhaling, exhaling, then inhaling, inhaling, exhaling, in order to absorb more oxygen than with normal breathing. This technique was also used to quickly adjust breathing after an intense workout.

走り方

　忍者は別名「早道之者」とも呼ばれている。手に入れた情報をいち早く伝えるために忍者は走ることもあったが、現代の走る感覚とは違って、早く歩く方法と考えればいい。

　走るときは遠くを見ずに近くを見て走る。あごが上がると呼吸が乱れて疲れるからだ。伊賀忍者が走るときの極意に「二重息吹」という呼吸法がある。「吸う・吐く・吐く」「吸う・吐く」「吸う・吸う・吐く」を繰り返すもので、普通の呼吸より酸素がたくさんとれる。これは激しい運動のあとに、すばやく呼吸を整えるためにも用いられた。

Jumping and Landing Methods

Ninja required a strong jumping ability to be able to leap walls and sneak into houses. There was a training method to increase leg strength by jumping out of a hole. First, ninja dug a shallow hole slightly wider than shoulder width, then climbed in, and jumped out. After a while, they dug the hole a little deeper to improve jumping strength. When jumping, try to bend the ankles and knees as little as possible, instead concentrate on training the toes.

Alternatively, ninja would often have to jump from high places. Even ninja were afraid of jumping from heights. When jumping from high places, the ninja would crouch, and lower their eyes to relieve any fear. To soften their landing they used not just their legs, but both hands too, like a cat. These jumping techniques are extremely dangerous and should never be imitated.

跳び方と降り方

塀に飛びついて家に忍び込むなど、忍者にとって強いジャンプ力は必須だ。脚力をつけるために、穴から跳び出す鍛錬法がある。肩幅より少しだけ広い穴を掘り、その穴に入って跳び出すというものだ。最初は穴を浅く掘り、脚力のアップとともに穴を深くしてゆく。足首や膝の屈伸もできるだけ使わずにジャンプすることで足の指が鍛えられる。

いっぽう、忍者は高い所から飛び降りることもあった。忍者といえども高い所から飛び降りるのはこわい。そこで飛び降りるときにはしゃがんで目線を低くして恐怖心をやわらげた。また、着地の際は、足だけでなく両手も使い、ネコのようにふわりとやわらかく着地した。これらの飛び降りる技はきわめて危険なため、けっしてまねしてはならない。

Fire Handling Methods

A great danger for ninja in the mountains was being attacked by wild animals such as bears, boars and the now extinct Japanese wolf. Therefore, when camping, they tried to keep a fire burning all night. Ninja knew not only how to light fires, but knew how to use fire well.

One way was to cook food. The raw rice was wrapped in a *tenugui* cotton towel, soaked in water for about half a day, then buried in the soil, and a campfire was made above it. Depending on the intensity of the campfire, rice can be cooked in about an hour. Another method is to move the bonfire before bedding down, and sleeping on the warm ground. This is called *jigotatsu,* or the earth heater technique.

火の利用法

　山中で野宿する場合、いちばん危険だったのはクマやイノシシ、いまは絶滅したニホンオオカミなどの野生動物に襲われることだった。そのため野宿するときはひと晩中たき火を絶やさないようにした。忍者はただ火を燃やすだけでなく、火をうまく利用する方法を知っていた。

　1つは飯を炊くこと。生の米をてぬぐいで包み、水に半日程度浸してそのまま土に埋める。その上でたき火をすると、火の強さにもよるが、1時間くらいで飯が炊ける。もう1つは寝るときにたき火を動かして、温まった地面の上に寝る。これを「地ごたつ」という。

Searching for Drinking Water

It is said that humans can survive for about a week without food or water. When traveling through the mountains, the ninja carried a bamboo canteen and always replenished it at springs or valley rivers. If water was difficult to obtain, they would use the following skills to find some.

1) Stick some feathers in the ground. After several hours, if water droplets have formed on the feathers, then water is nearby. 2) Spread a *tenugui* cotton towel in a cave. The next day, if the towel is damp and heavy, then water is nearby (left page). 3) Dig a hole about a meter deep and press your ear to the ground. If there is groundwater, the sound can be heard. 4) Ants nests are always located near water. Ninja also found groundwater by observing what plants were growing in certain areas.

飲み水の探し方

　人間は食べ物がなくても水があれば約1週間は生きのびられるといわれている。忍者は山の中を行くときには、竹で作った水筒を持ち歩き、谷川や湧き水があったら補給を忘れなかった。水がなくて困った場合は、次のような方法で水を探した。
　①鳥の羽を地面にさす。数時間たって羽に水滴がついていたら水が近くにある。②洞窟にてぬぐいを広げておく。次の日になって、てぬぐいが湿って重たくなっていたら水が近くにある（左ページ）。③地面を1mくらい掘って耳を当ててみる。地下水があれば音が聞こえる。④アリの巣があるところには近くに水がある。ほかに生えている植物を観察して地下水を探すこともあった。

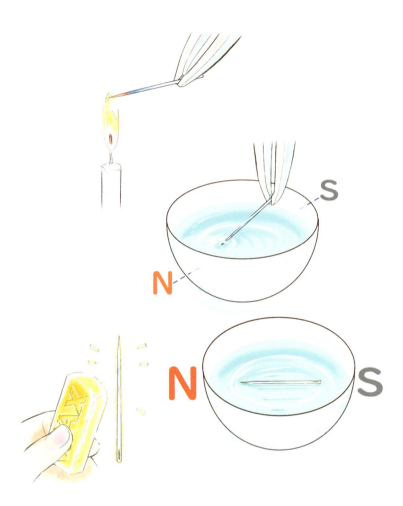

Determining Directions

The ninja were required to travel open roads, plains and mountains in order to reach their destination quickly and inconspicuously. At such times, it was imperative to have navigation skills so as not to get lost. The easiest way to determine direction was by noting the position of the sun during the day, and the position of the North Star at night, however this method was subject to weather conditions. While magnetic needle compasses were known, as they were rare in the Edo period, possessing one may have raised suspicions. Instead, the ninja would magnetize a sewing needle and use that.

This is how it was done. 1) Heat the tip of a needle until it glows red, then drop it in cold water. If the needle was cooled pointing north, it will show north, and if it was cooled pointing south, it will float with the tip pointing to the south. 2) Rub wax over the entire needle. 3) Gently lay the needle horizontally in a bowl of water so it floats.

方位を知る

忍者は、早く目立たないように目的地に着くために、抜け道や野山の中を進まなくてはならない。そのときに道に迷わないために方位を知る必要がある。いちばん簡単な方法は、昼間なら太陽、夜なら北極星の位置から方位を知る方法だ。しかし、天気が悪いと、この方法は使えない。方位を知るための道具として方位磁針があるが、江戸時代はまだ一般には普及していなかったため、持っていると怪しまれる可能性があった。そこで忍者は、縫い針を磁石に変えて使った。

作り方と使い方は次のとおり。①針の先を火で熱し、先が赤くなったら水につけて冷やす。針先を北に向けて冷やせば針先は北を向き、南に向けて冷やせば針先は南を向く。②針全体に蠟をこすりつける。③針を水面にそっと横たえて浮かべる。

Determining the Weather

Infiltration missions are best conducted on rainy and windy nights. The sound of footsteps is masked by the noise of the wind and rain, and the lack of moonlight improves chances of remaining unseen. It was important to know the direction of the wind when starting fires to confuse enemy camps, or setting fires to castles or buildings. For this reason, the ninja learned to read the weather in advance.

The ninja studied the basics of observing the stars, the moon and the clouds to understand the weather conditions. In the Iga and Koka regions, it was said that when the stars appear to flicker, the following day will see strong winds, and when the moon is veiled in a thin mist, it will rain the next day. Because the relationship between the weather and the sky differs regionally, if they were uncertain, they would ask a farmer or a fisherman about the weather forecast.

Additionally, they would observe bird movements to predict the weather. It was thought that rain would fall in the afternoon if hawks cried out in the morning, and that rain will fall later when crows splash themselves with water.

天気を知る

忍び込むのにいちばんいい天気は雨風が強い夜だ。雨や風の音に消されて足音が聞かれにくく、月明かりもないので見つかりにくい。また、敵陣に火をつけて混乱させたり、城などの建物に火をつけたりする際には、風が吹く方角を知ることが大事だ。そこで、忍者は前もって天気を知る術を身につけていた。

天気を知るために星、月、雲の様子を観察することは基本。伊賀・甲賀地方では、星の光がチカチカとまたたいているときは、翌日は風が強く、月がうすい「かさ」をかぶっているときは翌日に雨が降るといわれた。天気と空の関係は地域によって違うため、知らない土地に行った場合は農民や漁師に天気の予測を聞いた。

ほかに、天気を予測するために鳥の動きも観察した。朝にトンビが鳴いたら午後は雨、カラスが水をあびると雨になるといわれた。

Determining the Time

In order to meet with associates and act in unison, it was necessary to set approximate times, and so the ninja had various ways of telling the time.

The basics of the seasonal movements of the sun, and the times of sunrise and sunset were understood. In order to know the time at night, they looked at the positions of the seven stars forming the "Big Dipper", the direction of which changes so as to become a way to tell the time.

Another way of telling the time unique to the ninja was known as the "Cats Eye Clock". It was a method based on the natural changes in the size of a cat's pupils depending on the brightness. However, it wasn't always accurate, being affected by weather and location.

時刻を知る

仲間と待ち合せて複数で行動するときは、おおよその時刻を決めておく必要があるため、忍者は時刻を知る方法を身につけていた。

日中であれば太陽の位置で時刻を知った。季節によって違う太陽の動きや、日の出や日の入りの時刻を心得ておくのは基本だ。夜の時刻を知るには北斗七星を探した。7つの星で「ひしゃく」を形づくる北斗七星は見つけやすく、時間とともに「ひしゃく」の向きが変わるため、時刻を知る目安になった。

忍者ならではの時刻を知る方法として「猫の目時計」がある。明るさによってネコの瞳の大きさが変わるという性質を利用した方法だが、天気や場所に影響されるためいつも正確とは限らない。

Yaei-jutsu
(Field Operation Techniques)

When ninja made camp, they chose the position well. The main points considered for a location included: 1) Choosing a spot under a leafy tree in preparation for sudden rain or night dew. 2) Avoiding areas with venomous insects. 3) Avoiding riverbanks, valleys and hollows as even small rivers can suddenly flood. 4) Avoiding locations where rock fall is a possibility.

In order to protect themselves from the rain and dew, ninja would make a simple tent called a *nochu-no-maku*, out of a *haori* jacket (p. 112). Even in camp, the ninja remained highly alert, and would not sleep deeply. When they did sleep, they laid left side down. This was done to protect the heart, and to be able to use weapons with the right hand freely if they came under sudden attack.

野営術

忍者が野宿するときは、場所をよく選んだ。場所選びのおもな注意点をあげよう。①夜露や突然の雨に備えて、葉のよく繁った木の下を選ぶ。②毒虫のいそうなしげみは避ける。③小さな川でも突然増水することがあるので、河原や谷間、水がたまりそうなくぼ地は避ける。④落石がありそうなところは避ける。

忍者は雨や夜露を防ぐために、羽織(p.112)を使って「野中の幕」という簡易テントを作った。こうして野営する際も、油断なくつねにまわりに気を配り、深く寝入ることはなかった。横になって寝る場合は必ず左側を下にした。突然、襲われて斬りつけられても心臓を守れるし、右手ですぐ武器も使えるからだ。

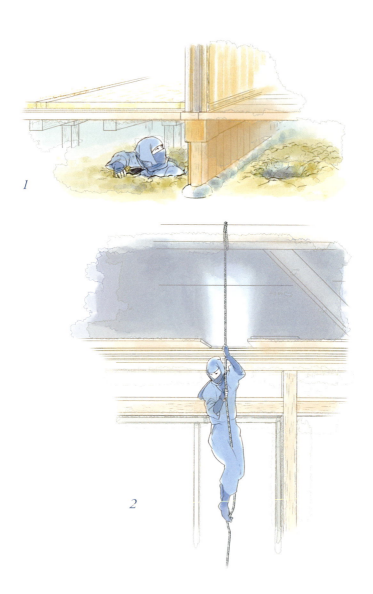

Shinnyu-jutsu
(Intrusion Techniques)

Ninja would infiltrate castles and mansions to obtain secret letters and documents, and to eavesdrop in order to secure information. Naturally, other group members would act as a lookout, and provide diversions. The ninja must therefore elude the enemy to successfully complete their mission. This is an introduction to the art of intrusion.

The Ground Spider Technique: mine a tunnel from outside the premises, and sneak into the site. Foundation Hole Technique: dig a hole in the earthen foundations of a house and crawl in under the floors (1). Roof Hole Technique: make a hole in the outer roof, so as to access and hide between the roof and the ceiling space. Descending Spider Technique: using a rope (*nawa*, p. 112), the ninja could descend from the ceiling into a room (2).

Ninja could also enter a premises through a small window. Providing the space was big enough for the ninja's head to fit, he could then dislocate his joints such as the shoulders in order to get through.

侵入術

密書（秘密の手紙や書類）を手に入れたり、密談を盗み聞きしたりするために、忍者は城や屋敷に忍び込んだ。もちろん相手も見張りを立てたり、しかけを設けたりする。それらをかいくぐって無事に任務を達成しなければならない。ここでは屋敷への侵入術を紹介しよう。

穴蜘蛛地蜘蛛：屋敷の外から穴を掘って、敷地内に忍び込む。土台掘り：穴を掘って縁の下にもぐり、床下に忍び込む（1）。天蓋破り：屋根に穴を開けて、天井裏に忍び込む。下り蜘蛛：縄（p.112）を使い、天井から部屋へ降りる（2）。

小さな窓から侵入することもあった。頭が入る大きさの穴があれば、忍者は肩の関節をはずして通り抜けることができた。

1

2

Ongyo-jutsu
(Hiding Techniques)

In the times when ninja were active, moonless nights were so dark, you could not even make out the human form. The ninja would take advantage of this darkness, shrouding themselves in it, while executing their mission. The following are the main hiding techniques.

Kannon-gakure: hide like Kannon, the Goddess of Mercy. Crouch by a tree or wall and cover your face with the sleeve of your clothing (1). *Uzura-gakure*: hide like a quail. Cover yourself in a cape while blending in beside a large rock. *Tanuki-gakure*: hide like a raccoon. Climb a tree and conceal yourself in the foliage. *Konoha-gakure*: hiding under tree leaves. Hide amongst the fallen leaves and grasses. *Kitsune-gakure*: hide like a fox. Enter water, such as a pond, and conceal yourself amongst the water plants. Once covered in water plants, lie face up with your nose and mouth out of the water to breathe (2).

隠形術

忍者が活躍した時代、月のない夜は、人の輪郭も見えないほど暗かった。忍者はこの闇を利用して身を隠しながら仕事をした。おもな隠れ方には次のようなものがある。

観音隠れ：木や壁のそばにしゃがんで、装束の袖で顔を隠す（1）。ウズラ隠れ：大きな岩のそばで地にうつぶせ、体を丸くして身をひそめる。狸隠れ：木に登って葉の陰に身をひそめる。木の葉隠れ：草むらや茂みに隠れる。狐隠れ：池などの水の中に入り、頭に水草などをのせて隠れる。顔は上を向いて、鼻と口を水面から出して呼吸する（2）。

Intoku-jutsu
(Concealment Techniques)

Confidential documents and information recorded on paper had to be concealed and secreted home. The ninja had many ways of hiding such materials even if they were searched at a highway barrier checkpoint (*sekisho*, p. 113). One way was to twist the pieces together to form a long string, called *koyori*. This string was then woven into the strands of an *amigasa* straw hat (p. 113), or the braids of straw sandals, even sewn into a kimono lining for concealment.

The ultimate way to hide information was to shave your hair, then engrave the details into your head with a knife, like a tattoo. When your hair grows, it conceals the message, and upon reaching your destination your head is again shaved, and the information divulged. A ninja could only use this technique once in a lifetime, and this tactic should never be imitated.

隠匿術

密書など紙に書かれた秘密情報を得た場合、それを隠して持ち帰らなければならない。忍者は、関所 (p.113) で持ち物を調べられた場合でも見つからないように隠す方法を考えていた。密書を端からひねって紐状の「こより」にするのも1つの方法。こよりを編み笠 (p.113) やわらじなどに織り込んだり、着物に縫い込んだりして隠した。

究極の隠し方は、髪の毛を剃って刃物で頭に文字を刻み込む方法だ。入れ墨の一種といってもいい。髪が伸びたら髪を整えて情報提供先に向かい、そこで髪を剃って文字を読んでもらう。忍者が一生に一度しか使えない技であり、絶対にまねしてはいけない。

Touso-jutsu
(Escape Techniques)

The ninja's most important role was to bring back any information obtained. When the ninja became aware of the enemy, he hid first, and when confronted with detection, considered escaping. Fighting was the last resort for a ninja.

When escaping, they would scatter 3-4cm tetrahedron-shaped spiked seeds (2) or metal caltrops, known as *maki-bishi* (1). These caltrops would stop the enemy's pursuit, stabbing through their straw sandals and into the soles of their feet. They were often set out on the escape route in advance.

In *ninjutsu*, such escape measures are known as *tonpo*, while collectively they are called *goton-sanjippo*. Refusing to give up, the ninja would use anything available to aid their escape, including animals, gunpowder, natural assets such as trees, grasses and other forms of nature, even the elements, such as weather, fire and water.

逃走術

忍者にとって最大の使命は、得た情報を持ち帰ることだ。忍者は敵に気づかれそうになったときはまず隠れ、万が一見つかったときは逃げることを考えた。忍者が戦うのは最後の手段なのだ。

逃げる際に使うのが「撒き菱」という方法。約3〜4cmの大きさの天然のヒシの実(2)や、先の尖った金属で作った「鉄菱」(1)を撒く。わらじやぞうりで踏むと足の裏に刺さって敵の動きを止めることができる。撒き菱はあらかじめ逃走路にしかけておくことが多い。

逃げるための忍術を「遁法」といい、数々の遁法をまとめて「五遁三十法」と呼ぶ。天候、木、草、火、水などの自然、人や動物、火薬など、まわりのすべての物を利用して、忍者は最後まで諦めずに逃げるのだ。

Henso-jutsu

(Disguise Techniques)

The ninja employed *nanabake-no-jutsu*, seven main disguises, to allow them to travel incognito anywhere across the country. For example, when disguised as a monk, it wasn't enough to only adopt the clothing, but also to acquire the occupation's unique skills and language. The seven main disguises were the following.

A *shounin* (merchant): a traveling peddler selling sweets or medicines. A *yamabushi* (mountain ascetic): disguised as a *yamabushi*, a ninja would not raise suspicions when crossing mountain paths (2). A *komusou* (itinerant Buddhist monk): zen monks who wander the countryside, their faces conveniently hidden under woven basket-like headgear, and playing *shakuhachi* flutes (p. 114) (1). A *houkashi* (entertainer): performers such as magicians, acrobats, monkey trainers and other street entertainers. A *sarugakushi* (performer): a traveling artist who performs song and dance acts. A *soryo* (priest): as a monk, a ninja can enter a temple where information can be readily obtained. A *tsune-no-kata* (itinerant worker): an ordinary traveler not bound to a particular occupation.

変装術

忍者は「七化けの術」という、全国どこを旅しても怪しまれない職業に変装した。ただ外見を装うだけでなく、僧侶に変装する場合は読経することができるなど、その職業ならではの技や言葉づかいまで身につけていた。七化けの術の職業は次のとおり。
行商人：薬や飴などを売り歩く商人。山伏：各地の山を歩いて修行する人。山の中で行動していても怪しまれない (2)。虚無僧：禅宗の一派に属する僧で、深い編み笠と尺八 (p.114) がトレードマーク。編み笠で顔を隠せることが利点 (1)。放下師：手品、軽業、猿回しなどの芸人。猿楽師：各地を回って歌や踊りを見せる芸人。僧侶：情報がたくさん集まる寺に出入りすることができる。常の形：職業にとらわれないふつうの旅人の姿。

Henso-jutsu
(Appearance Changing Techniques)

The techniques of changing the appearance of one's face are called *henso-no-jutsu*. The most important techniques are: 1) Change the color of the skin using a dye. 2) Inflate cheeks with wads of cotton. 3) Cause inflammation and swelling to your face by deliberately applying allergens such as plant saps and natural poisons. 4) Grow the hair and beard to give the appearance of being ill. 5) Fit large fish scales over eyes to appear as though blind.

The techniques of changing body shape and image were known as *hentai-no-jutsu*. Usually people tend to ignore the sick and physically handicapped, and so the ninja would fast to look ill, carry a walking stick, even dislocate joints to look disabled.

They would also employ the technique of *hensei-no-justu*, a voice changing technique.

変相術

　顔を変える術を「変相の術」という。おもなものを紹介しよう。①おしろいや染料を使って肌の色を変える。②口に綿などをふくんで、頬をふくらませる。③毒草の汁を顔に塗ってわざと顔をはれさせる。④髪やひげをのばして病人に見せる。⑤魚のうろこを目に入れて瞳を曇らせて、目の不自由な人に見せる。
　体の形やようすを変える術を「変体の術」という。ふつう、人は病人や身体の不自由な人に対しては気をゆるめて警戒しないので、忍者は断食して痩せて病人のふりをしたり、杖をついたり肩や足の関節をはずして身体が不自由な人を装ったりした。
　そのほか、「変声の術」という声を変える術も使った。

Joho Dentatsu-jutsu
(Information Transmission Techniques)

If the ninja had neither time nor opportunity to meet and communicate with his companions, the following predetermined signals and rules allowed them to pass on information.

Noroshi (smoke signals, left page): rising smoke could be used to communicate information to friends at a distance. The secret to making smoke rise straight up, high into the sky, was to mix some Japanese wolf dung into the gunpowder. *Tako* (kites): a red kite signals the start of an operation, a yellow kite means abort, and so on. The color of the kite signifies the action to be taken. *Ishi-oki* (placement of stones): stones left along a road in a predetermined arrangement could communicate information to companions arriving later. *Yui-nawa* (rope knots): *nawa* (ropes) were hung inconspicuously from places such as the eaves of a home, and information was conveyed by way of the knots. *Hata* (flags): information was transmitted by use of flags.

情報伝達術

仲間に会って伝える時間のない急ぎの連絡は、あらかじめ決めておいたルールにしたがい、合図にして伝える。

狼煙：煙を上げて、遠いところにいる仲間に情報を伝える（左ページ）。煙をまっすぐに高く上げる秘密は、火薬の中にニホンオオカミのフンをまぜること。凧：赤い凧が揚がったら作戦開始、黄色い凧は作戦中止など、色によって内容を決めておく。石置き：いくつかの石を、あらかじめ決めておいた置き方で道に置き、あとから来た仲間に情報を伝える。結縄：軒先などに縄をぶらさげ、結び目の形で情報を伝える。旗：旗をふる動作で情報を伝える。

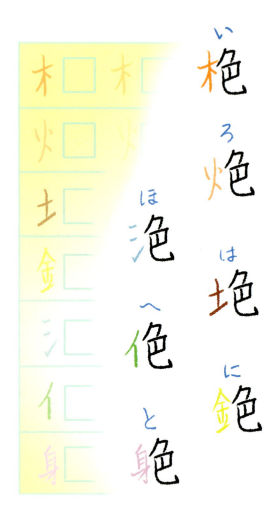

いろ は に ほ へ と
桍 炮 垉 泡 俹 鉋 皰

Ango-jutsu
(Encryption Techniques)

The ninja often used encryption when communicating complex information to their team. These codes were changed regularly so as not to be read by the enemy. Ninja of Iga and Koka used original writing called *shinobi iroha*. A combination of 49 various written characters including those for wood, fire, earth, gold, water, person, body, and so on were used in combination with color, blue, yellow, red, white, black, purple to make a code no one could read. The ninja knew to read only a certain line, such as the far left hand side, to understand the message.

It is also said that ninja used the ancient script known as *Kamiyo-moji*, for a code, as very few people were able to read it.

Sometimes, in place of written words or characters, rice dyed in five colors, red, blue, yellow, black and purple and known as *goshiki-mai* was used.

暗号術

忍者は仲間に複雑な情報を伝えるときは暗号を使い、万が一にも敵に見やぶられないように、そのつど暗号を変えることもあった。

伊賀・甲賀の忍者は、「忍びいろは」というオリジナルの文字を用いた。「木」「火」「土」「金」「水(氵)」「人(イ)」「身」をへんに、「色」「青」「黄」「赤」「白」「黒」「紫」をつくりにして組み合わせたもので49文字ある。

また、日本に漢字が入ってくる以前の文字といわれる「神代文字」は、読める人がほとんどいなかったため、忍者が暗号として利用したという。

文字のかわりに、「五色米」という赤、青、黄、黒、紫の5色に染めた米を組み合わせて文字を表すこともあった。

Kioku-jutsu
(Memory Techniques)

Important information obtained by a ninja infiltrating an enemy mansion or territory would not be written down as notes, but committed to memory. This is to avoid being caught if the memos are discovered at a highway barrier checkpoint.

Kioku-jutsu, the techniques of remembering, involve both imaging and association methods. The imaging method is as follows: create a multi drawered chest in your mind. Imagine writing the information on a piece of paper and place it in a drawer. When required, simply re-imagine which level and which number drawer the information you want was filed in.

The association method is a way to memorize numbers, by substituting them with body parts or food, making them easier to recall. For example, if 1=head, 2=forehead, 3=eyes, 4=mouth, 5=throat, 6=chest, 7=navel, then a difficult number such as 5234 is remembered as "throat, forehead, eyes and mouth". Touching or pointing to the part will further enhance recollection.

記憶術

　忍者は、屋敷などに侵入して得た重要な情報は、頭にしまい込んでメモなどはとらない。もし関所などでメモを見つけられたら捕まってしまうからだ。

　記憶術にはおもにイメージ法と連想法がある。イメージ法は、つぎのとおり。まず頭の中に引き出しのたくさんある箱を作り出す。そして、覚えたいことを頭の中で紙に書いて、箱の引き出しに入れる。必要なときに、「上から何段目、右から何番目の引き出しから取り出す」ことをイメージして思い出す。

　連想法は、覚えにくい数字などを体の部分や食べ物に置き換えて覚える方法。1=頭、2=ひたい、3=目、4=口、5=のど、6=胸、7=へそ、というように置き換え、5234という数字を覚えるときは「のど、ひたい、目、口」と覚える。その部分を自分で指さしたりふれたりしながら覚えるとよい。

Taijin-jutsu
(Interpersonal Techniques)

In order to obtain information possessed by the other party, it is necessary to get close to them and manipulate their heart and mind. This was called *taijin-jutsu*, interpersonal techniques, one of which was the *gojo-goyoku-no-kotowari*, or "principle of the five emotions and five desires". Most people experience five driving emotions and desires, and by understanding and taking advantage of their emotional needs and desires, the ninja could manipulate people as required.

The five emotions are joy, anger, sadness, comfort and fear. By pleasing your target, angering them and causing them to make a misjudgment, sympathizing with them, or scaring them, basically you can move your opponent in a way convenient to you.

The five desires include food, sex, fame and prestige, assets, such as property or possessions, and luxury. You can further gain control of such people by stimulating their greed, by for example talking about money making schemes.

対人術

相手が持っている情報を得るためには、相手に近づき、その心をあやつる必要がある。これを対人術といい、その1つに「五情五欲の理」がある。人には5つの感情（五情）と5つの欲求（五欲）があり、人がどんなときにどんな感情や欲求を持つかをよく知ることで、自分の思うように人を動かしたり自分に従わせたりする術である。

五情の理とは、喜怒哀楽恐の5つ。相手を喜ばせたり、怒らせたりして判断力をにぶらせたり、同情させたりこわがらせたりして相手を自分の都合のいいように動かす。

五欲の理とは食、性、名声、財産、風流の5つ。金もうけの話をもちかけるなど、相手の欲を刺激して自分の意のままにあやつる。

Seishin Toitsu-jutsu
(Concentration Techniques)

Ninja trained their minds to remain calm and yet be able to respond immediately to any situation. One of the ninja's mental training methods was the *kuji-goshinho*, or "nine character self-defense method".

To remain calm and concentrate, they would recite nine words *Rin*, *Pyo*, *To*, *Sha*, *Kai*, *Jin*, *Retsu*, *Zai*, *Zen*, while making spiritual hand gestures, or moving the hand like a sword, in a way known as *shuto*. The *kuji-goshinho* would serve to encourage the ninja with the meaning, "When fighting, stand in the front lines!".

The *kuji-goshinho* would be chanted when the ninja found himself in a tight spot to remain calm, courageous and think clearly.

精神統一術

忍者はどんなときでも心を落ち着かせて行動できるように心を鍛えておく必要がある。忍者のメンタル・トレーニングのひとつが「九字護身法」だ。

心を落ち着けて集中し、「臨・兵・闘・者・皆・陣・列・在・前」という9つの文字を唱えながら、両手で印を結んだり（神仏の力を借りるために手で特定の形を作る）、手刀（手を刀に見立てる）を決められた形に動かしたりする。この9字は、「闘うときは最前列に立て！」と、自分を勇気づける意味がある。

ふだんから「九字護身法」を繰り返していると、ピンチのときにも九字を唱えることで冷静さをとりもどし、勇気と知恵が自然に湧いてくるようになる。

Kunoichi-no-jutsu
(Female Ninja Techniques)

Female ninja were called *kunoichi*. Female ninja did not undertake the same difficult missions as the men due to their differing physical strengths and physique. Instead they would seek a position such as a maid within a castle or mansion in order to conduct their missions covertly. If employed within the manor, they would become familiar with the room layout, and possibly hear important information in the gossip of the other maids. They could also use their sexuality to get close to the samurai of the mansion, and by making them fall in love and letting their guard down, the *kunoichi* could gather information from them. *Kakuremino-no-jutsu* was the practice of a covert *kunoichi* working as a maid, who would bring a chest of belongings into the mansion which in actual fact contained a male ninja hidden inside.

Naturally, the female ninja undertook weapons training and disciplined their bodies so as to defend themselves in emergency situations.

くノ一の術

くノ一とは女忍者のこと。女忍者は体力や体格の違いから、男忍者と同じことはしなかったが、男忍者では難しい仕事を担当した。その仕事の代表が、女中として屋敷や城に勤めて秘密を探ることだ。いつも屋敷にいれば間取りもわかるし、女中同士の噂話から重要な情報を聞き出すこともあった。また、女の色気を使って屋敷の侍に近づき、相手が自分に惚れ込んだところで情報を聞きだすこともあった。「隠れ蓑の術」といって、女中として忍び込んだ女忍者が荷物を取り寄せ、その荷物の中に男忍者が隠れて忍び込んだりもした。

もちろん、女忍者はいざとなったときに自分の身を守れるように武器の練習や体の鍛錬を行っていた。

Secrets of the Ninja House

Despite the often-called *ninja yashiki* or ninja houses containing defensive features, most ninja lived in ordinary farming homes. Often the houses were designed to protect the secrets hidden inside from falling into enemy hands, such as the confidential scrolls depicting composition and production of gunpowder, as well as gunpowder itself. When rival ninja entered the home, a variety of concealment places and escape doors provided the ninja with opportunities to run or hide.

Doors disguised as walls or flooring called *kakushi-do* were used to hide people and featured small peep holes so those hidden could see what was going on (left page).

Tsuri kaidan were special stairs that led to a mezzanine floor or space between the ceiling and roof. When raised by a drawstring after climbing, they resembled a shelf inside an alcove.

忍者屋敷の秘密

　敵の侵入を防ぐしかけがある屋敷はよく「忍者屋敷」と呼ばれるが、多くの忍者はふつうの農家と同じ家に住んでいた。しかけを備えた家は、火薬そのものや、火薬の材料の調合具合などを書いた忍術伝書などを隠しておいた家で、敵の手に渡ってはいけない秘密を守るために作られた。ライバルの忍者が忍び込んできたときに隠れたり、持ち出して逃げたりする時間をかせぐために住まいにいろいろなしかけを作った。

　人が隠れるためのしかけは、「隠し戸」（左ページ）が代表。壁や床が戸になっていて内側に隠れたり、外への抜け穴が作られていたりした。

　中二階や屋根裏の隠し部屋に上るための「つり階段」は、棚に見える部分が留め金をはずすと階段になるしかけだ。

Photo: Ninja Museum of Iga-ryu　写真提供：伊賀流忍者博物館

There were many hiding places known as *mono-kakushi* inside the ninja house, places such as outer edge floorboards that could be raised, and secret papers, etc. buried in the earth below it. Stepping or pressing on the end of a particular floorboard would spring it open to reveal a hidden sword ready for use (left page). Hollowed pillars could conceal hiding places too.

There were many such houses in the famed ninja villages of Iga and Koka, each containing all manner of devices, however, very few of these ninja houses remain to this day.

忍者屋敷の中には物を隠すためのしかけも作られた。「ものかくし」は、縁側の床板の一部が開くようになっていて、地面を掘って密書などを置き、上から砂などをかけて隠すしかけ。「刀隠し」(左ページ)は、床板のいっぽうの端を踏んだり押したりすると床板が跳ね起きて、中に隠した刀を取り出すしかけ。そのほか、柱をくりぬいて中に物を隠したりした。

忍者の里として有名な伊賀や甲賀にはかつて忍者屋敷がたくさんあった。しかけの種類や数はまちまちで、それぞれの家が工夫していた。現在、忍者屋敷はほとんど姿を消している。

Chapter 3

Ninja Tools

第三章

忍者の道具

Shinobi Shozoku
(Shinobi Costume)

It was imperative that ninja attire remained inconspicuous. Ninja would often wear field farm work clothes, as they worked the land in between missions. Regular farming wear was easy to move about in, and would not have aroused suspicion. Being close fitting, it made it harder to get snagged when infiltrating narrow spaces.

The *shinobi* costume was not dyed black, but was usually a deep indigo blue (*ai*, p. 115). During the dying process, it was immersed in an iron-rich liquid, the unique smell of which would act as a viper and insect repellant. In addition, brown and gray costumes were also worn, depending on the location and brightness. The wear was often reversible, with a different color on the inside, so that a quick change transformed the ninja's appearance. The many pockets inside the jacket carried medicines, fire lighters and items to be protected from the wet.

忍び装束

　忍者の服装は目立たないことが第一だ。忍者は、忍者の仕事がないときは農作業をしていたので、ふだんは農作業着＝野良着を着ていた。野良着は身体にぴったり合っているので動きやすいし、人に怪しまれない。それに、狭い所から忍び入るのに引っかかりにくい。

　忍び装束の色は黒ではなく、藍（p.115）で染めた濃い紺色が一般的だ。さらにクレ染め（鉄分を含んだ液体に浸して染める）にして、独特のにおいで野山ではマムシや虫を除ける効果もあった。また、茶色や灰色の装束もあり、場所や明るさで使い分けた。表と裏で色が違う装束もあり、見つかったときに急いで表と裏をひっくり返せば、別人に変身できる。上着の内側にはいくつもポケットがついていて、薬や火種など、濡れては困る物を入れた。

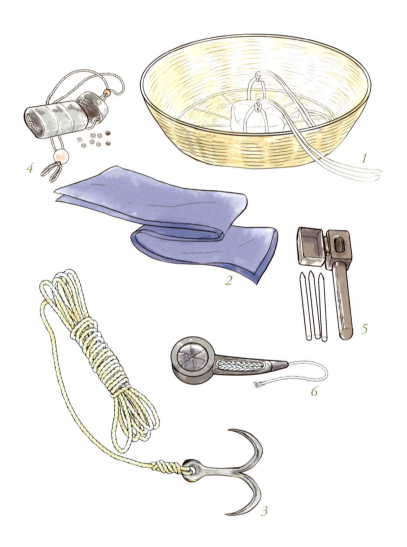

Shinobi Roku-gu
(Six Essential Tools of Shinobi)

The ninja would always have the necessary tools prepared and ready for travel as they were expected to depart as soon as a mission was assigned. These were known as the "Six Essential Tools of *Shinobi*", and consisted of the following.

An *amigasa* (woven straw hat): protect from the sun and rain, also to conceal one's face (1). A *tenegui* (cloth towel): approximately 1m in length. This multi-purpose cloth could be used as a *zukin* (p. 115) or head cowl, as a belt, a water filter, and so on (2). A *kaginawa* (grappling hook and rope): used to capture and bind the enemy, to secure a boat or raft to a pier, or pull things from the water (3). Medicines: including self-treating stomach remedies and medicines for wounds, also poisons to be used on the enemy (4). *Sekihitsu* and *yatate* (writing instruments): the *sekihitsu* was made of hardened clay and similar to modern day chalk. The *yatate* was a portable set of inkwell and brush (5). *Hidane*: a fire starting device, like a modern-day lighter (6).

These common travel items were also carried by the general public, and so they would not arouse suspicion should the ninja's belongings be checked.

忍び六具

忍者は任務を命じられるとすぐに旅立たなくてはならないために、つねに旅に必要な道具を揃えておいた。それが以下の「忍び六具」といわれる物だ。

編み笠：雨よけ、日よけになり、顔も隠せる(1)。三尺てぬぐい：長さ約1m。頭巾(p.115)、帯がわり、水をこすなど、活用方法は多い(2)。鉤縄：敵を縛って捕まえたり、舟やいかだを桟橋に固定したり、水の中のものを引き上げたりする(3)。薬：傷薬や腹薬など自分のために用いるほか、敵に用いる毒薬などもある。印籠に入れていた(4)。石筆・矢立て：筆記用具。石筆は粘土を固めて焼いた、チョークのようなもの。矢立ては筆と墨がセットになったもの(5)。火種：いまのライターのようなもの(6)。

これらは一般人も用いた旅行用品だ。荷物検査をされても怪しまれないように、忍者はありふれた道具を応用して使っていたのだ。

Shuriken
(Throwing Stars)

Shuriken were small weapons made of iron, and thrown at an enemy. The proper terminology for a *shuriken* throw is a "strike". *Shuriken* are divided into two types, the *heiban shuriken* flat steel plate type and the spike-like *bo shuriken*, and each have a variety of forms.

Shuriken are seen as the iconic weapon of the ninja, however, ninja rarely used *shuriken*. The reasons are: 1) Being a specialized weapon, carrying one would be deemed suspicious. 2) They were heavy and cumbersome. 3) They were expensive, being custom made by a blacksmith. 4) They were ineffective unless used at close range, and even then their lethality was limited.

A ninja would only use a *shuriken* as a last resort when confronted by an enemy. The *shuriken* would be used to make a diversion allowing escape, or to cut the opponent down with a sword.

手裏剣

　鉄で作られた小型の武器で、相手めがけて投げて使う。手裏剣を投げることを正式には「打つ」という。手裏剣の形は平べったい「平板状手裏剣」と細長い「棒状手裏剣」に大きく分かれ、それぞれさまざまな形がある。

　手裏剣は忍者が用いる代表的な武器と思われがちだが、じつは忍者は手裏剣をあまり使わなかった。その理由は、次のとおり。①特別な武器なので持っていると怪しまれる。②重くてかさばる。③鍛冶屋に特注しないといけないので金がかかる。④近い位置で使わないと威力がなく、また殺傷能力も低い。

　忍者が手裏剣を使うときは、相手と向かい合ってどうしても助かりたいときだけだ。手裏剣を打って相手がひるんだすきに逃げたり、刀で斬りつけたりした。

Katana

(Japanese Sword)

Swords used by the ninja were no different from the swords used by the samurai. An unusual or non-conforming sword would only raise suspicion at barrier checkpoints. The sword was always worn on the left hip, and with a slight twist of the hip, drawn by the right hand while the left hand held the scabbard. In places where the ceiling is low, such as an attic space, or under a floor, the sword was carried on the back across the left shoulder.

What was important to the ninja was how the sword was used. They mastered swordsmanship techniques to allow them to fight effectively in confined spaces, such as indoors. Additionally, they would use the "Seven *Sageo* Techniques". The *sageo* is the braided cord tied to the scabbard to hold it in place and is about 2.7m long. One of the techniques was the *zasagashi* technique, in which the scabbard was balanced on the tip of the sword, with the *sageo* cord held in the mouth while walking in the dark (left page). When the scabbard touched the enemy, the scabbard was immediately discarded and the ninja was ready to fight. Additional techniques, such as using the *sageo* to entwine spears and block the enemy's movement, were wide and varied.

刀

　忍者が使う刀は、侍が使う刀と変わりはない。特別な形の刀を持っていたら関所などで調べられたときに怪しまれてしまうからだ。刀は必ず右手で抜いたので左腰に帯び、左手で鞘をおさえ、右手で柄を握って腰をひねって刀を抜いた。屋根裏や床下などの天井が低いところでは左肩から斜めにして背中に背負う。

　忍者にとって重要なのは刀の使い方だ。部屋の中など狭い所でも自在に戦えるような剣術を習得した。また、「下げ緒七術」といわれる刀の応用術を使うこともあった。下げ緒とは刀を腰に帯びるために鞘につけてある紐のことで長さは約2.7mある。その中の1つ「座さがし」（左ページ）は、鞘を刃先までずらして下げ緒を口にくわえて暗闇を歩く方法で、鞘に敵がぶつかったらすぐに鞘をはずして戦うことができる。そのほか、下げ緒を槍にからめて敵の動きを封じるなど、下げ緒の応用術は広い。

Giso Buki
(Disguised Weapons)

In many cases, ninja used weapons disguised as common tools to deceive the enemy. For example, the *shikomi-zue* resembled a simple walking cane, that concealed a blade or a *fundou* weighted chain (left page). Naturally, so as not to draw suspicion to having such an item, the ninja would have to disguise himself as an old man using a walking stick.

There are also instances where musical instruments such as flutes and the bamboo recorder-like *shakuhachi* contained blades or were used as *fukiya* (p. 116) In order to carry such items, it was necessary to be able to actually play the instruments. Other weapons disguised as ordinary items included *tessen* folding fans of iron, *kogai* women's decorative hair pins, or blades concealed inside *kiseru* (p. 116). It was important to not only disguise the concealed weapon, but also to not arouse suspicions as to why the item is being carried.

擬装武器

　忍者は敵をあざむくために、ありふれた道具に武器を仕込むこともあった。たとえば杖の中に刃物や分銅（金属の重り）のついた鎖を仕込んだものが「仕込み杖」（左ページ）だ。ただし、老人に変装するなど、杖を持っていても怪しくないようにしなければならない。

　ほかにも笛や尺八などの楽器に刃物や吹き矢（p.116）を仕込むこともある。これらを持ち歩くには、実際にその楽器を演奏できるようにしていないとばれてしまう。そのほかの擬装武器としては、「鉄扇」という金属製の扇に見せかけたものや、女性の髪飾りである笄や喫煙具のきせる（p.116）に刃物を仕込んだものもある。擬装武器は武器を隠す工夫だけでなく、その道具を持っていることを怪しまれないことが大切なのだ。

Kama and Kasugai
(Sickle and Clamps)

Ninja used unobtrusive tools as weapons. The *kama* sickle is representative of such weapons. The sickle was a common agricultural tool used for harvesting rice and weeding. Being a sharp bladed tool, it made an ideal weapon, and with the attaching of a weighted chain, it became an even more powerful *kusarigama* apparatus (1). The weight at the end of the chain was directed at the enemy, and while thrown off guard or entwined in chain, the enemy was then attacked with the sickle.

Kasugai clamps (2) are staple-like bracket shaped nails for coupling timbers. When held in the middle, they could be used as a weapon. They could be thrown in place of a *shuriken*, and come in handy when scaling the stone walls of a castle. They were also used to break doors and locks when infiltrating. Large nails known as *gosunkugi* (about 15cm long) were used in the same way as the *kasugai*.

鎌とかすがい

忍者は持っていても怪しまれない道具を武器にした。その代表が鎌やかすがいだ。鎌は稲刈りや雑草刈りなどに用いるごくふつうの農具。切れ味が鋭いので、そのままでも強力な武器になるが、鎌に分銅のついた鎖をつけた「鎖鎌」(1) にするとより威力が増す。鎖鎌は分銅を敵に投げ、ひるんだ隙に鎌で攻撃するのが一般的な用い方。

かすがい (2) は材木どうしをつなぐ「コ」の字形の一種の釘。棒の部分を握って武器として使った。また、投げれば手裏剣がわりになり、城の石垣を登るときにも便利。忍び入るときに戸や鍵を壊すのにも使った。五寸釘（約15cm）という長い釘もかすがいと同様に用いた。

1

2

Tekkokagi, Tekken and Kakute
(Claws, Knuckle Dusters and Spiked Rings)

The *tekkokagi* claws (1) are not unique ninja weapons, but rather a development of agricultural tools used for grass mowing. They were used like the claws of a tiger or a bear to slash an opponent, or when attacked to block and disarm the enemy and take their sword.

The *tekken* is a steel weapon featuring a ring for four fingers and with spikes and blades around it. There were other hand weapons, such as *kakute* (2). Shaped like a ring with sharp spikes, *kakute* were developed from a farm tool for weeding. Because it was small, it was difficult for the enemy to see in the dark. By gripping the enemy's hand while wearing a *kakute*, and sinking the spikes into their flesh, you could induce enough pain for them to drop their swords.

These hand weapons were most effective in close combat. Even without a sword themselves, ninja had the necessary weapons and skills to fight off an opponent.

手甲鉤、鉄拳、角手

「手甲鉤」(1) は、本来は草刈りに用いる農具だ。手甲鉤を武器として使えば、相手にトラやクマの爪で引っかかれたような傷を負わせた。また、敵の攻撃を受けたり、鉤で敵の刀を引っかけて奪いとったりもできる。

「鉄拳」は輪に指を4本通して使う金属製の武器で、外側に角があるものと刃がついているものがある。手につける武器ではほかに、指にはめて使う「角手」(2) がある。指輪に歯がついたような形をしており、これも草刈りのための農具だ。小さいため暗いところでは敵から見えづらい。角手で敵の手をつかめば、歯が肉に食い込んで刀を落とすほどの激痛を与えることができる。

これらの手につける武器は接近戦で効果がある。忍者は刀を持っていなくても小さな武器で敵と戦う技術を身につけている。

Fukiya and Fukumibari

(Blowguns and Blow Darts)

Fukiya (1) were steel needle blow darts partially wrapped in *washi* paper (p. 117) and shot from a blowgun disguised as a flute. Poison would be applied to the tip. *Fukumibari* were needles spat at the eyes of the enemy directly from the ninja's mouth. With practice, several could be let loose at once, and greater momentum could be achieved than when using a blow tube.

The ninja used strong triangular cross sectioned needles called *sanryoshin* (2). The needles were small and easy to carry, and unlikely to raise suspicions even if discovered. If used in close quarters, the offensive force was greater than the *shuriken*.

吹き矢とふくみ針

吹き矢 (1) は、笛に見せかけた吹き筒に、和紙 (p.117) を巻いた針を仕込んで吹く。針には毒をぬる。ふくみ針は針をそのまま口にふくんで吹いて飛ばす。慣れると一度に数本飛ばすことができ、近距離から敵の目を狙う。

忍者が使った針は「三稜針」(2) という断面が三角の丈夫なもの。針は小さくて携帯しやすく、見つかったとしても疑われにくい。接近戦で使えば攻撃力は手裏剣よりもはるかに上だ。

Kaki
(Fire Devices)

Because many covert missions took place in darkness, the ninja used various light sources and fittings. Among the variations were many hand-held fire lit torches, called *taimatsu*. The ninja of Iga and Koka had abundant knowledge of the uses and manufacture of gunpowder, and often used it for lighting.

Tools using gunpowder were called *kaki*. Some of the most powerful weapons in the ninja's arsenal were firearms and explosives. The mixture and amount of gunpowder used in a matchlock gun, or *hinawaju* (p. 117), determined the range and effectiveness of the weapon (left page). The *hyakuraiju* was a series of loud firecrackers, set off to fool an enemy into thinking they were being fired upon by a corps of gunmen. Additionally, *hiya* fire-arrows were gunpowder filled bamboo tubes attached to arrows, *horihiya* were hand thrown grenades, and *uzumebi* were landmine-like weapons buried in the soil which exploded when stepped on.

火器

　忍者は夜に行動することが多かったため、さまざまな照明器具を使った。照明の中でも松明（松の脂を燃料にして、火をつけて手で持つ照明）はさまざまな種類がある。照明には火薬を用いることも多く、伊賀や甲賀の忍者たちは、火薬の豊富な知識を持っていて、自分たちで火薬を作っていた。

　火薬を使う道具を火器という。火器には武器もあり、忍者の武器の中でも最強の威力を発揮した。火薬を使った鉄砲の「火縄銃」（左ページ、p.117）は火薬の調合法によって弾の飛距離が変わった。爆竹を大きくしたような「百雷銃」は大きな音を発して、敵に鉄砲隊が来襲したと思わせた。ほかに、火薬をつめた竹筒を先端につけた「火矢」、手投げ爆弾の「放り火矢」、土に埋め、踏むと爆発する「埋め火」などもある。

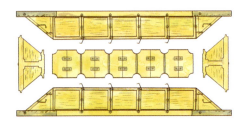

Suiki
(Water Devices)

Castles often had water filled moats around them to prevent enemy invasion. Ninja would choose a moonless, or new moon night to infiltrate such castles. First a ninja would quietly swim the moat, once the guards were dispatched other ninja would follow employing devices called *mizuki*. *Kameikada* were rafts made from bamboo and wood frames and using large empty ceramic jars as flotation devices. *Gamaikada* were bundles of reeds tied intermittently with wooden planks set at cross angles through them for stability. *Tsuzura* rafts were made from woven reed baskets. These *hasami-hako-bune* could be disassembled for carrying (left page).

Many people believe the ninja walked across water using large circular flotation devices called *mizugumo* (lit. water spider), but this device is not a *mizuki*. In fact, *mizugumo* will not float, but sink. They were used to cross natural muddy wetlands.

水器

城のまわりには敵の侵入を防ぐために水堀がめぐらされていることが多い。忍者は城に忍び込む場合、月明かりのない新月の夜を選んだ。まず敵に見つからないように静かに泳いで水堀を渡って見張りを倒したら、続く者たちは水器を使って堀を渡った。水器には竹や木を格子状に組んだいかだに空の甕を挟んで浮かせる「甕いかだ」、蒲を束ねて横から板をさし込んだ「蒲いかだ」、つづら(草を編んで作った箱)を浮力にした「つづらいかだ」、分解して持ち運べる「挟箱船」(左ページ)などがある。

忍者が使う水を渡る道具というと、丸い大きな下駄のような形をした「水蜘蛛」を思い浮かべる人もいるだろう。じつはこれは水器ではない。実際に「水蜘蛛」を使って水を渡ろうとしても沈んでしまう。これは、自然の湿地帯を利用した泥の堀を渡るための道具である。

Toki

(Climbing Devices)

Ninja would train their fingers especially to be able to climb the stone walls of a castle with their bare hands. They would also use *gosunkugi* nails and *kasugai* clamps, fitted in between the gaps in the stones to help them climb. As one of them would climb, he would insert tools to allow easy access for his comrades. These were known as *toki,* climbing devices.

A ladder is an inconvenient and conspicuous item when carried fully assembled. For that reason, the ropes and parts were carried separately before being assembled on site. Depending on the fabrication method, there are various types of ladder, such as the *musubi-bashigo*, the *tobi-bashigo*, the *kumo-bashigo* and others. *Nawa-bashigo* were ladders made of rope and were easy to carry (left page). A four-pronged boat anchor-like grappling hook was tied to the rope and thrown to catch onto a roof or wall for climbing. Knots called *wasa* were tied at equal intervals to make climbing easier.

登器

忍者はふだんから指を鍛えており、素手で城の石垣を登ることができた。また、五寸釘やかすがいを石垣の石と石のすきまにねじ入れながら登ることもあった。ひとりが石垣の上に登ったら、後続の忍者たちがすばやく登れるように道具を使うこともあった。それが登器だ。

登器の代表がはしごと縄だ。はしごは組み立ててあるものを運ぶと不便だし目立ってしまう。そこで棒と縄をばらして運び、現地で組み立てた。組み方によって、「結びばしご」「飛びばしご」「雲ばしご」などの種類がある。「縄ばしご」(左ページ)は縄だけでできたはしごで、持ち運びやすい。鎌を船の碇のように4本重ねて縄をくくりつけたものを投げ、屋根や塀に引っかけて登る。縄に「わさ」と呼ばれる結び目を等間隔に作っておくと登りやすい。

Ninja Rations

Because of the demands of their work, ninja required a healthy and strong body, and were always careful about their diet. Ninja ate a balanced diet of nuts, soybeans, cereals, wheat, brown rice and so on, and were careful about their weight. They believed that eating black foods would make them stronger and so they ate black soybeans, black rice, black sesame seeds, brown sugar etcetera.

When on secret missions, the ninja carried the following rations: *hoshi-ii* (1) is steamed, dried rice which could be eaten as is, or softened in water or hot water. *Kikatsugan* were small balls of various ingredients including ginseng, buckwheat flour and yams. *Suikatsugan* used to prevent thirst were made from pickled plum and sugar crystals. Eating these increased saliva, in turn quenching thirst. *Katayaki* (2) were hard, baked biscuits of ground brown rice and wheat flour, and are sold even now as a souvenir of Iga, known as the birthplace of ninja.

忍者の食事

忍者の仕事は健康で丈夫な体でなければ務まらないので、日頃から食事には十分に気をつけていた。木の実、大豆、雑穀、麦、玄米などをバランスよく食べ、体重があまり増えないように注意した。また、黒いものを食べると元気が出ると考え、黒大豆、黒米、黒ゴマ、黒砂糖などをよく食べた。

忍者の仕事をするときは、次のような携帯食を持参していた。「干し飯」(1)は米を蒸したあとに干したもので、そのまま食べられるほか、水や湯でやわらかくして食べた。「飢渇丸」は朝鮮人参、そば粉、ヤマイモなどさまざまな材料をまぜて小さく丸めたもの。「水渇丸」は梅干しの果肉などに氷砂糖をまぜて作ったもの。食べると唾液が出てきて、のどの渇きをいやした。「かた焼き」(2)は玄米や小麦を粉にしてかたく焼いたもので、忍者の里で知られる伊賀ではいまもお土産として売られている。

Appendix

Glossary

Ninja Villages to Visit

付録

用語集
訪ねてみたい忍者の里

Glossary | 用語集

Introduction

Shinobi

Shinobi is the native and historical reading of the kanji 忍, meaning perseverance or patience. It is also the original title by which ninja were known. Other names for the ninja included *shinobi-no-mono*, *monomi*, *nokizaru*, *rappa*, *kusa* and *Iga-mono* amongst others. "Ninja" itself is a relatively new word and does not appear in the antique manuscripts of the time. *Shinobi* are described as covert agents, mercenaries and spies involved in espionage, deception and guerilla warfare.

Sengoku Period

A time period of Japanese history, defined as being between 1467 and 1615, and characterized by continual military conflict between various warlords, political intrigue and social upheaval. The Sengoku period, also known as the Warring States period, was initiated by the Onin War (1467-1477) and ended with the Siege of Osaka in 1615, when Tokugawa Ieyasu cemented his control by removing all potential competition

はじめに

忍び しのび

しのびとは漢字の忍の読み方であり、忍耐や、他人に気づかれぬように隠れるという意味がある。また、忍びとは忍者そのものを指す。忍者の名称には、「忍びの者」「物見（ものみ）」「軒猿（のきざる）」「乱破（らっぱ）」「草」「伊賀者（いがもの）」などがあった。「忍者」という呼び名は比較的新しい言葉であり、忍者が活躍した時代の史料には登場しない。忍びとは、現代でいえば、諜報活動やゲリラ戦で活躍する秘密組織のスパイや傭兵ということができる。

戦国時代 せんごくじだい

日本の歴史の一時代で、「戦国大名」と呼ばれる領主たちが戦争を繰り返した激動の時代。「応仁の乱」（1467～77）から織田信長が室町幕府の将軍を追放した1568年までの時代をいうのが一般的だが、始まりと終わりの時期には諸説ある。織田信長の死後に豊臣秀吉が1590年に全国を統一していったん戦乱は終結するが、豊臣秀吉の死後に徳川家康と豊臣秀頼（秀吉の子）が対立。

with the destruction of the Toyotomi clan.

Edo Period

A time period of Japanese history also known as the Tokugawa Period after the ruling Tokugawa clan, and taking its name from their castle in Edo, now modern-day Tokyo. Defined as being between 1603 and 1868, the period was characterized mostly by relative peace, extensive public works, economic stability, an elaborate feudal and Confucian based social hierarchy, and development of the arts and culture all the while under strict Tokugawa rule. During the Edo period, a rigid national isolationist policy was enforced, preventing Japanese from leaving the country, and foreigners from entering.

1615年、「大坂夏の陣」で徳川家康が豊臣氏を滅ぼして、全国支配を確立した。

江戸時代 えどじだい

江戸時代は、「徳川時代」とも呼ばれる。日本の歴史の1603〜1868年で、武士の徳川家が全国を統治し、徳川家の主は「将軍」と呼ばれた。将軍の居城が江戸（現在の東京）にあったことが名の由来。江戸時代の社会は儒教に基づいた封建制。天下泰平で、経済や芸術・文化が発展した。徳川家の厳格な支配のもとで、鎖国政策がとられ、日本人が外国に行くことと外国人が日本に来ることを禁じた。

Chapter 1

Daimyo

Powerful feudal lords with extensive hereditary domains and armies of samurai. Edo period *daimyo* were allocated the authority to govern their territories by the shogun, and in return were subjected to control through the *Sankin Kotai* system, whereby their families were to remain in Edo, ostensibly as potential hostages, while the *daimyo* were forced to travel back and forth between their domains and Edo, to provide alternate-year mandatory attendance services including administrative, policing and guard duties at the shogun's castle.

第一章

大名 だいみょう

広大な領地を統治し、多くの家来を持つ封建領主。江戸時代には、将軍から1万石(1石は成人が1年に食べる米の量に相当する)以上の所領を与えられた武士を大名と呼んだ。江戸時代の大名は、妻子を江戸の屋敷に常駐させて、1年おきに江戸と領地を行き来する「参勤交代」が定められていた。大名は江戸に滞在する期間、江戸城にいる将軍に拝謁したり、江戸城で催される儀式に参列したりすることが公務だった。また、幕府の役職につく大名もいた。

Tokugawa Ieyasu
(1542-1616)

Founder of the Edo Shogunate. Born the son of the *daimyo* of Mikawa province (eastern Aichi prefecture). Held hostage by the Oda clan between the age of six to nine, then from nine to nineteen by the Imagawa clan, he was finally free following the death of Imagawa Yoshimoto at the Battle of Okehazama. He allied himself with Oda Nobunaga, and unified Mikawa. His powers were expanded under Nobunaga, and he submitted to Toyotomi Hideyoshi's authority on the death of Nobunaga. Accepting the Kanto region from Hideyoshi as his fief, he based himself in Edo Castle. Upon the death of Hideyoshi, the nation returned to civil war status, and, in 1600, Ieyasu claimed victory in the decisive Battle of Sekigahara, after which he assumed the position of Shogun. In 1615 he solidified his authority by attacking Osaka Castle and destroying the last remnants of the rival Toyotomi clan.

徳川家康
とくがわいえやす
(1542～1616)

江戸幕府の初代将軍。三河（現在の愛知県東部）の大名の子として生まれる。6歳から19歳まで、織田家や今川家の人質となる。桶狭間（おけはざま）の戦いで今川義元（よしもと）が死ぬと今川家を離れ、織田信長と同盟して三河を統一。信長とともに勢力を拡大するが、信長の死後に豊臣秀吉に服従。秀吉の天下統一にともなって関東を領有することとなり、江戸城を居城とする。秀吉の死後、1600年の関ヶ原の戦いで、天下の主導権を握って将軍に就任。1615年に大坂城を攻めて豊臣氏を滅ぼし、江戸幕府を盤石のものとした。

Bakufu

Japan's feudal military government, the head of which was the shogun, hence also being known as a shogunate. Subordinate to the imperial court, various *bakufu* existed between 1185 and 1868. Literally translated as "Tent Government" based on the notion of a temporary war camp, the *bakufu*, via the shogun and through military means held almost absolute military and administrative control of the nation. A total of 39 men held the official title of shogun within three *bakufu*, the Kamakura, Muromachi and Edo *Bakufu*. Many of the medieval shogun were cloistered or puppet shogun, as they were merely hereditary figureheads with actual political power manipulated from behind the scenes.

幕府 ばくふ

「将軍」を長とする日本の武家政権。戦場で将軍の陣営に幕を張ったことが名の由来といわれる。天皇や貴族が政治を行う「朝廷」に代わって、1185年〜1868年まで「鎌倉幕府」「室町幕府」「江戸幕府」の3つの幕府が政治の実権を握った(幕府が途絶えた時期もある)。計39名にのぼる幕府の将軍の多くは、政治の実権を握った家臣によって背後から操られる人形のような存在だった。

Tokugawa Yoshimune
(1684-1751)

Eighth Shogun of the Tokugawa *Bakufu*, ruling from 1716 until 1745, Yoshimune was the great-grandson of Tokugawa Ieyasu. Born into the Kii branch of the Tokugawa clan, one of three *Gosanke* hereditary houses from which a shogun could be chosen, he came to prominence following a series of deaths, first those of his father and two elder brothers which led to his appointment as *daimyo* of Kii (Wakayama prefecture), and then the early death of Shogun Ienobu, followed by his only son and heir, Ietsugu. As Ietsugu was too young to have a designated heir, Yoshimune was selected from the *Gosanke* as the next shogun. His almost 30-year rule was characterized by financial reform, and he is recognized as one of the most outstanding of the Tokugawa shoguns. Yoshimune is said to have brought his own ninja from Kii to operate as an elite unit upon becoming shogun.

徳川吉宗
とくがわよしむね
(1684〜1751)

江戸幕府の8代将軍(将軍在位1716〜1745年)。徳川家康の曾孫にあたる。徳川御三家(尾張徳川家、紀州徳川家、水戸徳川家の3家。将軍の後継ぎがいない場合は御三家から将軍が選ばれる)の1つ紀州徳川家に生まれる(紀州は現在の和歌山県)。父と2人の兄の死後に紀州徳川家を継いだ。6代将軍の徳川家宣(いえのぶ)が50歳で死に、その子の徳川家継(いえつぐ)が7代将軍に就任するが、幼くして亡くなった。家継は夭折したために後継者がなく、徳川吉宗が次の将軍として迎えられた。吉宗のほぼ30年間にわたる政治では、質素倹約や新田の開発などによって、幕府の財政の立て直しをはかった。吉宗の行った一連の改革は「享保(きょうほう)の改革」と呼ばれ、吉宗は徳川歴代将軍中の名君とされる。吉宗は将軍に就任する際に、紀州から忍者の精鋭部隊を連れてきたといわれている。

Oniwaban

An elite unit established by the Eighth Shogun, Tokugawa Yoshimune, engaging in undercover intelligence and security operations, reporting on the state of affairs in Edo and on news from around the country directly to the shogun. Other assignments included acting as staff within the shogun's inner palace, as guards of Edo Castle, administrators, gardeners, even manual laborers. Certain members were employed directly by Yoshimune to provide protection to high ranking officials, while others were sent to watch and obtain information on various *daimyo* and shogunate officials. The *Oniwaban* operated under a strict code of conduct that included preventing them from socializing with the general public, except when undercover. The name of the unit is believed to have either come from the *niwa*, or garden areas within Edo Castle where they were housed, or from their having undertaken gardening duties within the castle grounds so as not to attract attention.

御庭番 おにわばん

江戸幕府の8代将軍、徳川吉宗によって創設された役職。吉宗が紀州から連れてきた家臣によって組織された。江戸城の各所に配置されて警護にあたったが、その任務は表向きであり、諸大名の動静や江戸市中の風聞を探るための、吉宗直属の隠密（忍者）だった。彼らは江戸で大名や役人を監視するほか、ときには身分を隠して出張し、地方の実情を探ることもあった。御庭番の名は、江戸城の庭の番人として庭仕事に従事したことに由来するといわれる。

Chapter 2

Katana

The sword of the samurai, defined as a single-edged curved blade with a length greater than 60.6cm, forged with repeated folding of the steel to provide an exceptionally hard, keen edge. *Katana* were generally worn tucked into the *obi* sash, with the cutting edge facing upwards, rather than the similar *tachi* that was worn slung with the cutting edge downwards. *Katana* were often paired with a *wakizashi*, a shorter companion sword, together known as a *daisho* (long and short swords) and worn only by samurai.

第二章

刀 かたな

金属製の刃物で武士が武器として用いた。硬く、鋭い刃を作るために、鉄を何度も折りたたんで鍛造する。片刃のものを「刀」と呼び、両刃のものは「剣」と呼ぶ。一般的には、刃のある部分の長さが2尺 (60.6cm) 以上で、反りがあるものを太刀・刀という。いずれも鞘に納めて所持する。刀は刃が上を向くように腰の帯に差し、太刀は刃を下にして腰から紐で吊るして所持する。武士は、正装の際には、刀とともに「脇差」という短い刀をセットで所持し、この長短の刀の組み合わせを「大小」と呼ぶ。

Haori

A traditional hip or thigh length kimono-like jacket for men, usually worn over a *kosode* type kimono. The *haori* often featured the family crest on the left and right collar, and again on the upper central back area. It was worn either open, or loosely tied by chest high straps or *himo* strings hooked into special tabs inside the extended collar. During the Edo period, laws banning flamboyancy and public displays of wealth were enforced, and so the interior lining of many *haori* became lavishly decorated. *Haori* became fashionable for women in the early to mid 1800s.

Nawa

A vital utility tool used since pre-historic times, *nawa* rope was woven from rice straw or hemp jute. The twisted, braided strands of the *nawa* served to evenly distribute tension among the strands, creating a high tensile strength rope used in everything from construction and farming to maritime and military use. *Nawa* could be used for securing building timbers, attaching barrier posts, tying packhorses and prisoners, for climbing, tethering, carrying and pulling.

羽織 はおり

尻か太ももまでの長さの伝統的な日本の男性の衣服。洋装のジャケットのようなもの。通常は小袖のような着物の上から羽織る。胸のあたりにつけられた紐で前を結ぶが、結ばずに着ることもある。礼装の羽織には袖や背などに家紋を付けたものがあり、「紋付羽織」と呼ばれる。江戸時代、羽織は武士から庶民まで広がる。江戸時代に華美な服装を禁止する法令が出ると、裕福な人々は羽織の表地は地味にして、裏地を豪華に彩ることもあった。19世紀半ば以降から女性も羽織を着るようになった。

縄 なわ

わらや麻などの植物の繊維を縒って作った紐を、さらに縒り合わせて長くしたもの。先史時代から使われてきた、便利で必要不可欠な道具で、強度と張力にすぐれている。農業、漁業から軍用まで広く用いられ、人間が高い所に登ったり、物の運搬に使ったりするだけでなく、建築材を固定したり、区画を仕切ったり、家畜や囚人をつないだりすることにも使われてきた。

Sekisho

Sekisho were barrier checkpoints positioned along major roadways for the purpose of controlling the movement of people and weapons. Often a tax was collected by the guards at these checkpoints. During the Edo period there were 53 such *sekisho* situated along the five major highways leading in and out of Edo. Various passes called *tegata*, issued either by shogunate or domain officials, and by temples for pilgrims, were required for passage.

Amigasa

A broad-rimmed hat made of woven straw, reeds, or bamboo, usually conical in shape, they can also be domed, or wide flat-topped hats with a downturned brim. *Amigasa* were worn by a wide range of people, from peasants working the fields, to Buddhist priests and even samurai, and so wearing such headgear would not arouse suspicion. Worn primarily as shade from the elements, especially the sun and rain, *amigasa* could also be worn so as to conceal one's identity.

関所 せきしょ

通行する人と荷物を取り締まるために主要な道に置かれた検問所。江戸時代以前は関所を通る際に税金を徴収されることが一般的だった。江戸時代になると、江戸と各地を結ぶ主要幹線の「五街道」を中心として、全国に53の関所が置かれた。関所を通過する際には、「手形」と呼ばれる身分証兼旅行許可書の提示を求められることもあった。武士の場合は幕府または藩から公式な手形が出された。庶民の巡礼者は村や町の役人や寺院が手形を発行した。

編み笠 あみがさ

わら、葦（あし）、竹などで編んだ帽子。幅広で円錐形が一般的。ドーム型や、幅広で頂点が平らでつばが下がった形のものもある。陽の光、雨を遮るために使われる。編み笠は、農民、僧、侍など、幅広い層や職業の人々に使われたため、忍者が変装のために編み笠をかぶっていても怪しく思われなかった。編み笠の中はとても広いため、顔、秘密の文書、武器などを隠すのに使われた。

Shakuhachi

A five note-holed bamboo flute introduced to Japan from China in the 7th century. A *shaku* was an old unit of measurement about 30.3cm, divided into ten sub-units called *sun*. *Hachi* means "eight", and as the instrument's standard length was one *shaku*, eight *sun* (54.54cm) long, it became known as the *shakuhachi*. The instruments were played almost exclusively by men, in particular by the traveling Zen Buddhism monks of the Fuke sect.

尺八 しゃくはち

5つの穴がある竹でできた縦笛。7世紀に中国から日本に伝わる。「尺」はかつての長さの単位で1尺は約30.3cm。また、「尺」は「寸」という単位に分けられ、1尺は10寸。1尺8寸(約54.54cm)の楽器の長さが名前の由来となった。尺八は禅宗の一派である普化宗(ふけしゅう)の僧侶が儀式や布教の際に用いたことで知られる。

Chapter 3

Ai

A rich and distinctive dark blue natural dye prized for both its visual beauty as well as its more practical antibacterial qualities, the dye has been extracted from the *ai* plant and used for dying cloth, particularly silk, cotton and hemp for centuries. The art of *aizome*, dying cloth, became widespread particularly during the Edo period, when laws dictating the styles and fabrics to be worn were enforced, such as commoners not being permitted to wear silk, and extravagant colors and fashions being discouraged.

Zukin

A large cloth averaging 25cm in width and 2m in length, wrapped around the head to form a hood to conceal the face, in a way that allows for a small gap through which to see. The dark blue dyed *zukin* could also be used as a bandage if necessary, as a rope to bind a captured enemy, or to wrap items for carrying or concealment.

第三章

藍 あい

藍という植物から作られる品のある、独特なダークブルーの天然染料。見た目の美しさだけでなく、抗菌性と防虫という実用性も兼ね備える。絹、綿、麻などの自然由来の布を染色するのに長く使われてきた。江戸時代、庶民は高級な絹織物、派手な色の衣服を身につけることを法律で禁じられたが、藍染めは禁止の対象から外れたため、藍染の衣服は庶民の間に広まった。

頭巾 ずきん

顔や頭を覆い隠す布。忍者は、幅25cm、長さ2mほどの大きな布を使い、目の部分に小さな隙間を作るように顔や頭を覆った。忍者の使う藍染の頭巾用の布は、包帯や、敵を捕まえたり壁を登ったりするための縄や、ものを包んで運んだり、隠したりするためにも使われる。

Fukiya

Japanese *fukiya* blowguns were 50 to 120cm long tubes, used to project poison tipped darts. These *fukiya* had no mouthpiece, and so the user was required to seal the tube with his lips as he exhaled with force. Ninja are said to have used a slightly shorter blowgun, probably as a distraction more so than as a short-range weapon. The art of *fukiya* is now practiced as an international archery sport.

Kiseru

A Japanese tobacco smoking pipe, often with an elaborately engraved metal smoking bowl and mouthpiece, joined by a straight piece of wood or bamboo tubing in between. The bowl is smaller than a European styled pipe. Often ninja would disguise spiked or bladed weapons as the popular *kiseru*.

吹き矢 ふきや

50〜120cmほどの長い筒に、毒をぬった針を入れて勢いよく吹き出す。吹き矢にはマウスピースはなく、口で筒を覆い、呼吸の力で吹き出す必要がある。忍者は、長い筒を持っていると怪しまれるため、短めの吹き矢を使っていたとみられる。現在、吹き矢は的を射るスポーツとして国際的に普及している。

煙管（きせる）

刻み煙草（たばこ）を吸うための日本のパイプ。両端に金属製の火皿と吸い口があり、木または竹製のまっすぐな管で、火皿と吸い口をつなぐ。きせるが西洋のパイプと異なるところは、火皿が小さい点があげられる。忍者は突起物や刃のついたきせるを所持し、武器として使用した。

Washi

Strong, hand-made Japanese paper produced using the pulped bark fibers of the *kozo* (a type of mulberry), *gampi* or *mitsumata* bushes. The fibrous pulp is mixed with cold water and a sticky substance obtained from the roots of the *aibika* plant, then scooped onto a finely woven screen of reeds allowing the water to drain. The thin layer of pulp remaining creates a stronger, more durable and long-lasting paper.

Hinawaju

Matchlock guns were first brought to Japan by Portuguese sailors in 1543. The guns' firing mechanism included a fuse of smoldering rope, and so the weapons came to be known as *hinawaju* (lit. rope-burning guns) or *teppo* (lit. steel cannon). During the Sengoku period matchlock guns were mass produced across Japan.

和紙 わし

コウゾ、ガンピ、ミツマタの木の皮の繊維を原料にして作られる日本の伝統的な手作りの紙。木の繊維は、冷水と植物のトロロアオイの根から取れる粘液で混ぜられたのち、「簀（す）」（アシや竹で細かく編んだもの）ですくい上げて広く伸ばされる。簀の上に残った薄い紙の素は圧搾して水分を抜いたのちに乾燥させる。こうして完成した紙は、強く長持ちする。

火縄銃 ひなわじゅう

火縄によって火薬に点火し、弾を発射させるしくみの銃。1543年に九州の種子島（たねがしま）に漂着したポルトガルの船員によって伝来した。「火縄銃」「鉄砲」と呼ばれ、戦国時代に日本国内で大量に生産されて、合戦の戦い方を変化させた。

Ninja Villages to Visit ｜ 訪ねてみたい忍者の里

Ninja Museum of Iga-ryu

Located in Ueno Park, Iga (Iga City, Mie Prefecture) is known as a ninja village. The Ninja House is a reconstruction of the residence of the Iga clan. From hidden doors to compartments for hiding swords, every corner of the the residence is equipped with devices, and ninja and *kunoichi* provide guided tours with demonstrations. Among the main highlights are the Ninja Experience Hall, which displays many ninja tools, the Ninja Tradition Hall, where you can learn about *ninjutsu*, and a powerful ninja show. The *shuriken* throw experience (additional fee) is also popular.

伊賀流忍者博物館

　忍者の里として知られる伊賀（三重県伊賀市）の上野公園内にある。忍者屋敷は伊賀の土豪の屋敷を移築したもの。屋敷のあちこちに、隠し戸や刀隠しなどのしかけがほどこされており、忍者やくノ一（女忍者）が実演をまじえて案内してくれる。多数の忍具を展示する「忍術体験館」、忍術について学ぶことができる「忍者伝承館」のほか、迫力満点の忍術実演ショーなど、見どころいっぱいの施設。手裏剣打ち体験（有料）も人気だ。

Iga-ryu Ninja House
伊賀流忍者屋敷

Ninja Experience Hall
忍術体験館

Ninja Show
忍術実演ショー

Address: 117 Ueno Marunouchi, Iga City, Mie Prefecture
Phone: +81 (0) 0595-23-0311
Hours: 9:00-17:00 (Last entry 16:30)
Admission fee: 800 yen (Additional fee of 500 yen for the ninja show.)
Closed: December 29-January 1 (Other temporary closures are possible.)

―

住所：三重県伊賀市上野丸之内117
電話：0595-23-0311
営業時間：10:00〜16:00（入館は15:30まで）
入館料：1000円、忍術実演ショーは別途600円（休演日あり。要事前確認）
休み：12月29日〜翌年1月1日
URL: www.iganinja.jp

Koka Ninja House

Located in the southern Shiga Prefecture, Koka (Koka City, Shiga Prefecture) is a ninja village standing alongside Iga. The Koka Ninja House is the former residence of Mochizuki family, the head of the Koka ninja, and was built in the Genroku era (1688-1704). The interior has a three-story structure where you can freely observe and experience revolving doors, lookout windows, and pitfalls. There is also an archive room where ninja tools and *ninjutsu* literature are displayed. Fully enjoy the world of ninja with ninja herbal tea tasting (free), *shuriken* throwing (additional fee), and dressing up as a ninja (additional fee).

甲賀流忍術屋敷

　滋賀県南部の甲賀（滋賀県甲賀市）は、伊賀と並ぶ忍者の里。甲賀流忍術屋敷は甲賀流忍者を率いた望月氏本家の旧邸で、元禄年間（1688〜1704年）に建てられたもの。内部は3階構造になっており、どんでん返し、見張り窓、落とし穴などのしかけを自由に見学し、体験することができる。忍具や忍術伝書などを展示した資料室も併設。忍者飲用薬草茶の試飲（無料）、手裏剣投げ体験（有料）、忍者衣装変身体験（有料）など、忍者の世界を満喫できる。

Koka Ninja House
甲賀流忍術屋敷

Archive Room
資料室

Attic (3rd Floor)
屋根裏部屋 (3階)

Revolving door
どんでん返し

Trap 落とし穴

Address: 2331 Ryuhoshi, Konan-cho, Koka City, Shiga Prefecture
Telephone: +81 (0) 0748-86-2179
Hours: 9:00-17:00 (Last entry 16:30)
Admission fee: 600 yen
Closed: December 27-January 2 (Other temporary closures are possible.)

———

住所：滋賀県甲賀市甲南町竜法師2331
電話：0748-86-2179
営業時間：10：00〜16：30（入館は16：00まで）
入館料：750円
休み：毎水、第4木曜日、12月27日〜翌年1月3日（冬期休館、臨時休館あり。要事前確認）
URL: www.kouka-ninjya.com

黒井宏光　くろい ひろみつ

伝統忍者集団・黒党代表、日本忍術復興保存会会長。奈良県生まれ。大阪芸術大学映像学科卒業。大学卒業後に時代劇殺陣師に弟子入り。その後、甲賀流伴党21代目宗家・川上仁一氏に弟子入りし、忍術を学ぶ。1984年に伝統忍者集団・黒党を結成、日本はもとより海外でも公演を行っている。1985年に正しい忍術の普及を願い、日本忍術復興保存会を設立し、著作活動や講演等を活発に行っている。著書・監修に『忍者図鑑』(ブロンズ新社)など。

クリス グレン

オーストラリア出身、名古屋在住。ラジオDJ、タレント、翻訳者、英文ライター、インバウンド観光アドバイザー。戦国史に造詣が深く、訪れた城は550か所以上に及ぶ。NHK WORLD-JAPAN *SAMURAI CASTLES* などテレビ出演も多数。著書に『城バイリンガルガイド』(小学館)、『豪州人歴史愛好家、名城を行く』(宝島社)、『The Battle of Sekigahara』(Book Locker)がある。

岩﨑 隼　いわさき じゅん

マンガから水彩、油彩まで幅広く手がけるイラストレーター。実家は北海道小樽市の浄土真宗(三門徒派)専名寺。

編集協力
内田和浩

写真協力
黒井宏光　伊賀流忍者博物館
甲賀流忍術屋敷

装丁・本文デザイン
金田一亜弥　髙畠なつみ (金田一デザイン)

協力
日本児童教育振興財団 FAJE

Bilingual Guide to Japan
NINJA

忍者バイリンガルガイド

2019年12月15日　初版　第1刷発行
2025年 8月13日　　　　第4刷発行

著　者　黒井宏光
発行者　高橋木綿子

発行所　株式会社小学館
　　　　〒101-8001
　　　　東京都千代田区一ツ橋2-3-1
　　　　編集　03-3230-5118
　　　　販売　03-5281-3555

印刷所　株式会社DNP出版プロダクツ
製本所　株式会社若林製本工場
DTP　　株式会社昭和ブライト

編　集　矢野文子（小学館）

造本には十分注意しておりますが、印刷、製本など製造上の不備がござ
いましたら「制作局コールセンター」（フリーダイヤル0120-336-340）に
ご連絡ください。(電話受付は、土・日・祝休日を除く9：30～17：30)
本書の無断での複写（コピー）、上演、放送等の二次利用、翻案等は、
著作権法上の例外を除き禁じられています。本書の電子データ化などの
無断複製は著作権法上の例外を除き禁じられています。代行業者等の
第三者による本書の電子的複製も認められておりません。

©2019 Hiromitsu Kuroi, Jun Iwasaki, Chris Glenn, Kazuhiro Uchida
Printed in Japan
ISBN 978-4-09-388728-1

神社バイリンガルガイド
改訂版

加藤健司 監修

岩﨑 隼 画

小学館

English Renderings of Shinto Terms

This English and Japanese bilingual book introduces the basic knowledge and representative types of Shinto shrines.

Japanese terms are rendered in italicized Roman characters. The only diacritical mark used is the hyphen (-) to separate two adjacent vowel sounds.

Since the conventions for rendering these terms into English differ depending on the facility (shrine, temple, or public institute, etc.), terms used elsewhere may not be consistent with those used in this book. Given that even Japanese names and pronunciations of *kami* may differ depending on the sect or region, they cannot be generalized. Standard names are used in this book and are rendered so that they can be easily read by individuals who are not native speakers of Japanese.

本書の英文表記について

この本は、代表的な神社について紹介しています。日本語が母語ではない人のために、英語で訳してあります。

日本語はすべてローマ字読みにし、斜体のアルファベットで表記しています。発音は、母音が続いてしまう場合のみハイフン (-) を使用しています。

※これら外国語表記は、施設（社寺や美術館、公共施設、地方自治体等）ごとに異なるルールで表記されているため、本書と一致しない場合があります。特に祭神や祭礼の名称とその発音については、地方によって日本語でも異なることがあり、一般化はできません。本書では標準的な呼称を掲載し、外国語を母語とする読者ができるだけ平易に発音できる表記としました。

Table of Contents 目次

Introduction 6　　　はじめに

Chapter 1　　第一章
Visiting Jinja 11　　神社参拝

Torii 14　Sando 17　　　　　　　　　　鳥居　参道
Koma-inu 22　Shinshi 24　Haiden 26　　狛犬　神使　拝殿
Honden 32　Ofuda, Omamori 34　Omikuji 36　本殿　御札と御守　おみくじ
Ema 37　Engimono 38　Goshuin 40　　絵馬　縁起物　御朱印
Sessha, Massha 42　Chinju no Mori 44　　摂社・末社　鎮守の森
Shintaisan, Goshinboku 45　　　　　　　神体山・御神木

Chapter 2　　第二章
Kannushi and Prayer 47　　神職と祈り

Kannushi 49　Miko 52　　　神職とは　巫女
Norito 54　Shinsen 56　　　祝詞　神饌

Chapter 3　　第三章
Kami and Jinja 59　　神様と神社

Kami and Goshintoku 60　Matsuri 61　　祭神と御神徳　祭り
Ise Jingu 62　Izumo Oyashiro 66　　　伊勢神宮　出雲大社
Hachiman Jinja 68　Inari Jinja 70　　　八幡神社　稲荷神社
Kamo Jinja 74　Kasuga Jinja 75　　　　賀茂神社　春日神社
Tenmangu 76　Kumano Jinja 77　　　　天満宮　熊野神社
Sumiyoshi Jinja 80　Gionsha 81　　　　住吉神社　祇園社
Sengen Jinja 82　　　　　　　　　　　浅間神社
Munakata Jinja, Itsukushima Jinja 84　　宗像神社・厳島神社
Toshogu 86　Meiji Jingu 88　Kanda Myojin 89　東照宮　明治神宮　神田明神

Chapter 4　　第四章
Rites of Passage 91　　通過儀礼

Obi-iwai 92　Hatsumiyamoude 93　　　帯祝い　初宮詣
Shichigosan 95　Seijinsai 97　Kekkon-shiki 98　七五三　成人祭　結婚式
Yakudoshi 100　Toshi-iwai 102　　　　厄年　年祝い
Hatsumoude 103　Reitaisai 103　　　　初詣　例大祭

Appendix　　　　　　　　　　付録
Glossary 106　　　　　　　　用語集
Matsuri Festivals to Visit　　訪ねてみたい祭り
　Spring 118　Summer 120　　春　夏
　Fall 122　Winter 124　　　　秋　冬

Introduction

What is Shinto?

Simply put, Shinto is an indigenous Japanese folk religion, and has served as a foundation for thought, morality, and culture for Japanese people since ancient times. Today, when observing religious life in Japan, there is a phrase commonly used to express the Japanese approach to living with religions: "Japanese visit a Shinto shrine to pray at New Year, celebrate a wedding at a Christian church, and finally hold a funeral at a Buddhist temple."

This way of living is probably difficult to fathom not only for adherents of monotheistic religions such as Christianity, Judaism, and Islam, but also for polytheistic religions such as Hinduism. Some people might feel that ultimately, the Japanese lack a religious mind or a definitive faith in any religion. I would like to consider this seemingly contradictory Japanese approach to religious living.

はじめに

●神道とはなにか

　神道をひと言で要約すると、日本固有の民族信仰で、古くから日本人の思想や道徳、文化の基盤になっているものである、といえる。今、日本人の宗教的生活をみてみると、その信仰をあらわす言葉としてよく使われるものに、このようなものがある。「初詣は神社に行き、結婚式はキリスト教の教会であげ、葬式は仏教の寺でいとなむ」というものである。

　こうした行動はキリスト教やユダヤ教、イスラム教等の一神教の人々のみならず、ヒンドゥー教等の多神教の人々の目にも、日本人は本当はなにも信じていないのに信じているふりをしているだけと映るか、まったく理解しがたい信仰心をもった人間だと映ってしまうだろう。この矛盾に満ちた、といえる日本人の宗教的生活をどう考えるべきだろうか。

A highly tolerant religion

Firstly, it is evident that Shinto, the Japanese indigenous faith, is an extremely tolerant religion. Over many centuries, Buddhism and Christianity were accepted in Japan without conflict, although there was some political dissent, and this attitude formed a multilayered religion on the basis of Shinto tradition. Moreover, Japanese people never perceived or recognized the contradictions between religions.

This pluralistic approach to religion embodies the principles of Japanese tradition and culture. When examining the relationship between Shinto and Buddhism to understand this approach, consider that when Buddhism was introduced to Japan in the 6th century, Japanese people did not abandon their faith in Shinto even though Buddhism spread rapidly and became a major influence in Japanese society. Instead, what manifested was the syncretization of Shinto and Buddhism, to form a unique religion. Thus, the ideology of Shinto goes beyond standard religious dogma, and its principles coexist and are tolerant of other ideas and views.

●極めて寛容な宗教

　まず、日本固有の信仰である神道は極めて寛容な宗教であるということである。日本人は長い歴史のなかで、いくつかの政治的曲折があったものの、外来文化である仏教やキリスト教を受け入れてきた。そして、この態度は神道を基底に据えた、いわば重層的な信仰という様相を呈したものとなった。しかも、そうした宗教間の矛盾を感じず、あるいは気づかずにいたのである。

　このような多元論的立場が、神道を基盤にした日本の伝統的文化原理だといえる。こうした理解のうえで、たとえば神道と仏教の関係を考えてみると、6世紀に仏教が日本に伝播すると急速に日本に根を下ろし、多くの人々が帰依することとなったが、神道の神々に対する信仰を捨てることなく、神仏習合という特異な宗教形態を成立させることとなっ

Faith in supernatural energy

These principles apply not only to straddling different religions but also to a relationship with the natural world. Japanese mythology (*nihon shinwa*, p. 106) describes revered Shinto deities, *kami*. Some *kami* have the form of human beings and share the same emotions. There are many types of *kami*, including animals, plants, and all-natural phenomena such as ocean, mountains, wind, rain, thunder (*kantoki* in native Japanese), etc. All of these are objects revered in Shinto, acknowledging the divine spirits residing in supernatural energy in the natural world. It is believed that nature is a place where a soul or a spirit resides, and as such deserves reverence. This is why Japanese people have not felt compelled to conquer or expel nature.

た。このことからわかるように、神道は神学的教義を超えて、異なる宗教との相対化や共存を理念とするものであるといえる。
●超自然的な力を信仰
　この理念はなにも他の宗教との関係に限ったことではない。自然界との関係においても同様である。日本神話（p. 106）という古典に登場し、崇敬を受ける神道の「神」は人間と同じような姿をし、人間と同じように喜怒哀楽をあらわす。数多くのそうした神たちばかりでなく、神道では動植物のみならず、海や山、風雨雷（大和言葉でカントキという）といった自然現象にいたるまで超自然的な力に霊的なものを認め、それらを聖なるものとして信仰対象としてきたのである。それらには霊とか魂といったものが宿ると考えて畏敬の念を抱くことこそすれ、それらを駆逐、征服するなどという考えをもたなかった。

Unconsciously permeating the Japanese way of living

Shinto is deeply ingrained in day-to-day life, such as diet, clothing and shelter, so much so that Japanese often fail to even perceive it. Homes may have shrines to the *kami* of water in wells (there are still some families that use wells, although almost all have running water), or *kami* of ovens in the kitchen.

Also, rice farming is the main agricultural work in Japan, and is itself a sequence of Shinto rituals and events. From rice planting in spring to harvesting in autumn, farmers hold a number of festivities for *kami* of rice farming. Of course, they hold ceremonies for *kami* of rain in summer to pray for plenty of water and for *kami* of wind in autumn to pray for protection from typhoons.

●気づかないほど日本人の生活に浸透

さらに神道は、衣食住といった生活様式とも深い関わりをもっている。しかし、そのことはあまりに日常的すぎて、多くの日本人は普段はたいして気にも留めないほどである。家のなかを見てみると、台所には竈の神が、井戸(現在、家庭にはほぼ100％上水道が普及したが、今でも井戸をもっている家は少なくない)には水の神が祀られている。

生業においても、日本の農業の主体である稲作の農作業はほとんど信仰行事の連続といってよい。春の播種から秋の刈り入れまでの節目節目で、田の神に対して祭りを行う。もちろん夏には水の豊かであることを雨の神に祈り、秋立つ候には台風の来ないことを風の神に祈るのである。

Jinja, Shinto shrine as core of the community

Although *kami* were prayed for in nature, shrine buildings were constructed to enshrine them permanently at sacred places. These are referred to as *jinja*, which are scattered all over Japan. Religious communities were formed to honor *kami* enshrined in Shinto shrines, and various ceremonies were held throughout the year. Thus, Shinto shrines became the core of the community and provided a peaceful environment for people to aggregate in an ideological sense. Moreover, *jinja* are buildings that not only enshrine *kami*, but also encompass the surrounding forests and natural environment. In this sense, *jinja* are truly home for the Japanese mind.

Kato Kenji
Director of Tsurugaoka Research Institute

●村や町の中核となった神社

一方で、こうした神々を、霊地として神聖視された場所に恒常的に祀る施設が生まれた。これが日本の各地に点在する「神社」である。そして神社に祀られた神のもとに崇敬集団が形成され、年間を通じてさまざまな祭りが奉仕される。さらにこの神社が中核となって、人々の心安らぐ故郷としての村や町が理念的に形成されているといってもよい。また、神社は神々を祀る建物という建築的表示だけでなく、それを取り巻く森という自然環境をも含むものであって、日本人の故郷観の心象風景となっている。

（鶴岡八幡宮教学研究所所長　加藤健司）

Chapter 1

Visiting Jinja

第一章
神社参拝

Precinct of Shrine: Keidai

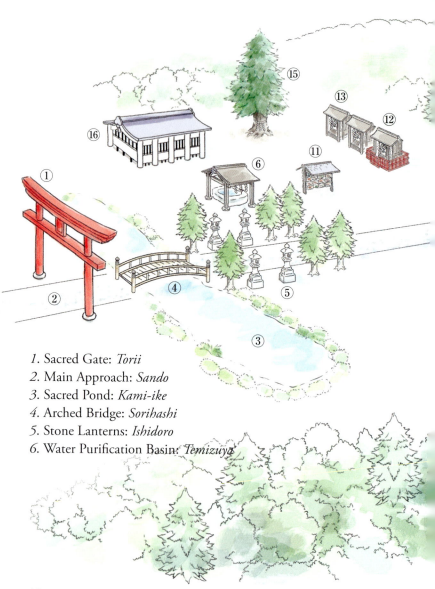

1. Sacred Gate: *Torii*
2. Main Approach: *Sando*
3. Sacred Pond: *Kami-ike*
4. Arched Bridge: *Sorihashi*
5. Stone Lanterns: *Ishidoro*
6. Water Purification Basin: *Temizuya*

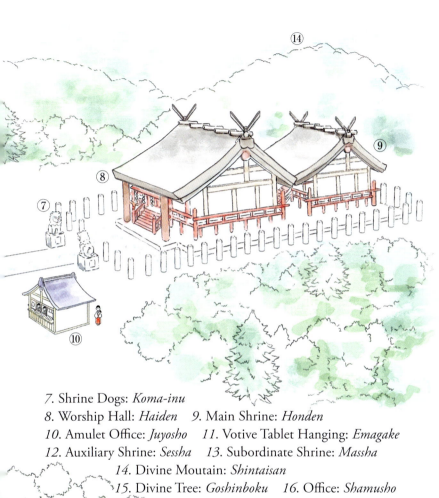

7. Shrine Dogs: *Koma-inu*
8. Worship Hall: *Haiden*   9. Main Shrine: *Honden*
10. Amulet Office: *Juyosho*   11. Votive Tablet Hanging: *Emagake*
12. Auxiliary Shrine: *Sessha*   13. Subordinate Shrine: *Massha*
14. Divine Moutain: *Shintaisan*
15. Divine Tree: *Goshinboku*   16. Office: *Shamusho*

境内の様子

①鳥居　②参道　③神池　④反橋
⑤石灯籠　⑥手水舎　⑦狛犬
⑧拝殿　⑨本殿　⑩授与所
⑪絵馬掛　⑫摂社　⑬末社
⑭神体山　⑮御神木　⑯社務所

Torii

A sacred gate called *torii* marks the entrance to a *jinja*, separating a Shinto sanctuary from the secular world and marking the entrance to a sacred world. Some visitors bow when they enter to pay respect. Some larger *jinja* such as *ichinomiya* (p. 107) have several *torii*.

Torii can be seen not only at *jinja* but also on mountains, huge rocks, or near waterfalls that are revered as divine objects. The presence of *torii* tells the visitor they are in a sacred place.

Although *torii* are now made of various materials, they were originally all wooden. The basic structure is two pillars with a top beam (*kasagi* ①) connecting them. Another crosspiece (*nuki* ②) is under the *kasagi*.

鳥居

鳥居は、神社あるいは社殿の出入り口として神聖な場所を示す象徴である。鳥居の先は神々の世界といってよい。そのため、一礼してから進む参拝者もいる。各地の「一宮」(p. 107)と呼ばれる大きな神社の長い参道には、しばしば複数の鳥居が立っている。

鳥居は神社ばかりではなく、山や大岩や滝など、古くから信仰の対象となった自然物の前にも立ち、その場が神域であることを示している。

鳥居の材質はさまざまだが、もともとは木造で、左右に2本の柱を垂直に立て、その上部に横柱(笠木①)を渡し、その下にも横柱(貫②)をつないで左右の柱を固定するのが基本形である。

This type of structure can be seen at Ise Jingu, and is called *shinmei torii* (p. 62). It is characterized by pillars that are rounded logs and *kasagi* and *nuki* made of square timber. When looking at it from the front, the appearance is linear. On the other hand, a common type called *myojin torii* (p. 14) has double *kasagi* with the ends raised. The pillars lean slightly inward, pierced by *nuki*.

Both types of *torii* have many variations. For example, *sanno torii* has a gable, and *ryobu torii* (p. 84) has a strut. *Senbon torii* (p. 70) is a line of *torii*, painted vermilion, that forms a sort of tunnel leading up to *jinja*.

伊勢神宮の神明鳥居 (p. 62) はこの形で、柱は丸材、笠木と貫に角材を用い、正面から見てすべて直線的に組み立てられる。これに対し、一般的な明神鳥居 (p. 14) は、笠木が二重で上部が両端にかけて反り上がっており、やや内側に傾いた左右の柱を貫がつらぬいている。

この両者にはともに変化形が多くある。また、破風をもつ山王鳥居や前後に控え柱をもつ両部鳥居 (p. 84)、群立する朱塗りの千本鳥居 (p. 70) など、個性的な鳥居も多い。

Sando

Originally, a *sando* was a way to approach the *jinja*. Nowadays, many shops and restaurants line the *sando*, but originally they were special streets where visitors purified themselves before entering *jinja* to offer prayers.

The center line of *sando* is called *seichu*, a pathway for *kami* to follow. Accordingly, visitors are asked to walk calmly and peacefully on the right or left side, taking care to show respect by avoiding the centerline as they approach the sacred place. Visitors can enjoy beautiful scenery along the *sando*, such as pine trees, cedar trees, cherry blossoms, sacred ponds, arched bridges, or vermilion colored two-storied gates.

参道

参道とは本来、参拝者が入り口である鳥居から神域へ入り、本殿などへ向かう通路を意味する。現在ではこの参道の両側に土産物屋が建ち並んでいたりするが、本来は神への祈りのために人々の心や身体を浄化するための空間であった。

参道は参拝のための道であるが、中央は正中といって神様が遷座の時に通る道である。だから人は真ん中を慎んで、左右の端を歩くようにする。神の気配を感じ取り、敬い、願い事をするために来たのだから、大声でしゃべったり、ふざけたりせず、静かに歩く。すると、さまざまな風景が目に入る。参道には松や杉や桜の樹木が立ち並ぶ。神池が静まり、太鼓橋が架かり、朱色の楼門が光り輝く。多数の苔むす石灯籠が出迎えてくれる参道もある。

Mossy stone lanterns, *ishidoro*, provide light for visitors along the way. Many were gifts from devout worshipers that date back to the Edo period (17th-19th century), while a few are even older, dating from the Heian period (8th-12th century).

Some *jinja* have more than one *sando*, usually called *omotesando* (front approach) or *urasando* (rear approach). There is a very famous street lined with luxury boutiques called Omotesando in Harajuku, Tokyo, so-named because it is actually the front approach to Meiji Jingu Shrine (p. 88).

　石灯籠は灯明をともして参道を照らすものだが、これらは神様への祈願のために信者から奉納されたものである。古いものでは平安時代、江戸時代のものは数多く残っている。参道では見るものすべてが清浄で、心が洗われていく。
「表参道」「裏参道」など、本殿へ至る参道が複数ある神社も多い。洗練された町として知られる東京の「表参道」は、明治神宮(p. 88)の主要参道の呼称がそのまま道路の通称として定着した例である。

Ritual of Purification: Temizu

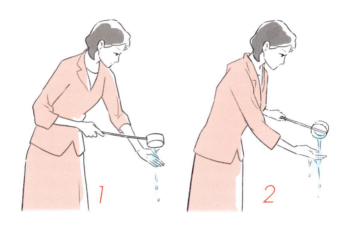

In Shinto, purity is respected above all else. Therefore, visitors are encouraged to conduct purification, *misogi-harae*, before proceeding to *jinja*. The water purification basin, *temizuya*, is a place for cleansing the mind and body. Visitors rinse their hands and mouth. This purification ritual, *temizu* or *chozu*, is a simplified form of the practices of *misogi* and *harae* followed in old times. *Misogi* was purification by ritual bathing, and *harae* was a way to remove impurities from one's clothing and accessories. *Kami* strongly avoid impurity (see *kegare*, p. 107) and welcome purity, so visitors purified themselves at rivers, spring

手水

　神道はなによりも清浄をモットーとする。したがって参拝者は神前に進む前に、「禊ぎ祓え」をすることが求められる。手水舎は、参拝者が手や口をすすぎ、心身ともに穢れ(p. 107)を洗い流す場所である。手水(てみず／ちょうず)は古くからの禊ぎ(水に体をひたして身を清めること)、祓え(穢れのついた服飾品を取り去ること)を簡略化したものである。神々は穢れを嫌い、清浄な者のみを受け入れるとされたため、人々は神域へ入る前に、近くの川や湧水、海で水垢離をした。その名残は、伊勢神宮を流れる五十鈴川に設けら

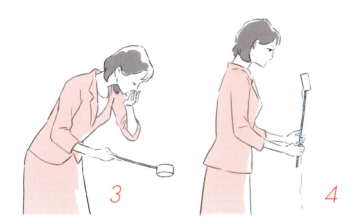

water or oceans before entering *jinja*. This tradition still remains at Ise Jingu Shrine where visitors use the Isuzugawa River for purification.

There is a simplified procedure for *temizu*. Pick up the ladle in your right hand and scoop up some water to wash your left hand (1). Transfer the ladle to your left hand and wash your right hand (2), then pour some water into your left palm to rinse your mouth (3). Let the remaining water run down the handle to clean it (4). The water basin area is sometimes small, so please share it with others and do not touch the ladle with your mouth.

れた石畳の御手洗場に見られ、今でもここで手を清める参拝者が少なくない。
　手水舎では、簡略化されたとはいえ一連の手順がある。右手で柄杓を取り、まず左手を洗い（1）、次に左手に持ちかえ右手を洗い（2）、また右手に持ちかえ左手のひらを使って口をすすぐ（3）。残った水で柄を洗い流してから、柄杓を元の位置に戻す（4）。手水舎は狭いため混雑している時も多い。互いに譲り合い、他の人も使う柄杓に直接口をつけないよう注意しよう。

Koma-inu

Along *sando* or around the worship hall, a pair of guardian figures, *koma-inu*, can be seen protecting the enshrined *kami* and warding off evil spirits. They have the bodies of dogs, but look more like lions (*shishi*). In the old days, shrines were guarded by a pair of *koma-inu* and a *shishi*. Generally made of stone, they commonly face each other, but some twist their body toward worshipers or face the entrance.

Typically, the dog on the right has an open mouth while the mouth of the one on the left is closed. This expresses the Sanskrit sound of "a" (meaning to start) and "un" (to end), and the sounds in pair symbolize the principle of the universe.

狛犬

　参道の入り口や拝殿の近くで見かける一対の狛犬は、進入する邪気を退け、祭神を守護する役目を担っている。「犬」といっても獅子の形態であるが、古くは獅子・狛犬が一対とされていた。参道の両脇から互いに向き合う配置のものが多いが、身体をねじって顔だけを参拝者に向ける形、社殿に背を向けて正面を向く形などがある。石造が一般的だ。

　典型的なものは向かって右側に口を開けた形「阿」を、左側に口を閉じた形「吽」を配置し、阿吽の対で一切万有の原理を示すといわれる。

Shinshi

Figures of dogs are replaced by other animals called *shinshi* in some *jinja*, but all are divine messengers of the enshrined *kami*. The foxes at Inari shrines (p. 70) are well-known. Hiyoshi shrines (p. 108) feature monkeys, Tenmangu shrines (p. 76) have oxes, and Kasuga shrines (p. 75) are guarded by deer.

Figures of hare are seen at Tsuki Jinja Shrine (Saitama), and the boars at Wake Jinja Shrine (Wake, Okayama and Kirishima, Kagoshima) stand as bravely as *koma-inu* to ward off evil spirits. At Mitsumine Jinja Shrine (Chichibu, Saitama), figures of the Japanese wolf (now extinct) are erected everywhere, and are believed to be helpful in warding off robbery and misfortune.

神使

　神社によっては狛犬ではなく、同様の役割を果たすほかの守護獣がいる。それらの動物は神の使いで、神使という。よく知られているのは、全国各地にある稲荷神社(p. 70)の狐。狐像は狛犬とほとんど同じ場所に置かれている。神使として日吉神社(p. 108)の猿、天満宮(p. 76)の牛、春日神社(p. 75)の鹿などが有名で、境内に像も設置されているが、狛犬のように建っているわけではない。

　そのなかで、調神社(さいたま市)ではウサギが、和気神社(岡山県和気町、鹿児島県霧島市)ではイノシシが狛犬のように建ち、けなげに邪気を防いでいる。三峯神社(埼玉県秩父市)では、絶滅してしまったが、かつては多く生息していたニホンオオカミ像が各所に建ち、盗難除けや災難除けの信仰を集めている。

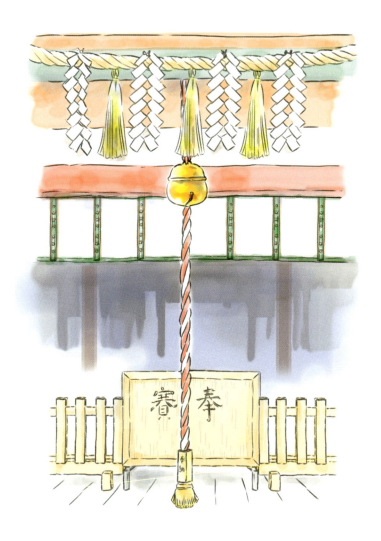

Haiden

After purification at *temizuya*, visitors proceed to the worship hall, or *haiden*, a place to offer prayers to enshrined *kami*. In old times, there was a sacred garden in front of the main shrine, and rituals were conducted there. A building functioning as *haiden* began to appear in the 9th century. Generally built in front of the main shrine, *haiden* are mainly used for rituals, but there are some *jinja* that do not have them, for example Ise Jingu Shrine (p. 62) and Atsuta Jingu Shrine (Nagoya, Aichi).

An offering box is placed in front of the *haiden*, and visitors toss in coins to show gratitude and offer prayers. The amount offered depends on the individual. Visitors should feel free to ring the bell rope. It is thought that the ringing possesses special energy to avoid misfortune and welcome divine spirits.

拝殿

手水舎で心身を清めたら拝殿に進む。拝殿は参拝者が神様に祈りを捧げる場所である。古くは本殿前の庭が祭典の場として使われ、9世紀ごろからこのような建物があらわれてきた。一般的には別棟の本殿の前に位置する。祭りを行うための場所として使用され、今日では多くの神社がこの設備をもつが、伊勢神宮 (p. 62) や熱田神宮 (愛知県名古屋市) のように拝殿が存在しない神社もある。

拝殿の前には賽銭箱が置かれている。参拝者はまずここにお賽銭を入れる。お賽銭は日々の平穏を感謝したり、お願いやお礼のために捧げるものだから、金額はそれぞれの判断でよい。乱暴に投げたりせず、心をこめて静かに入れよう。賽銭箱の上に鈴がつるされていたら、鳴らす。鈴は古代から神霊を招き、厄災を祓う力をもつとされている。

How to Pray

Toss in some coins, ring the bell, and then offer a prayer. When praying, visitors are encouraged to bow twice (1, 2), clap twice (3), then pray (4) and bow once more (5). This way of praying became common during the Meiji period (19th-20th century), but there are some exceptions, such as the Izumo Oyashiro Shrine (p. 66), which asks visitors to bow twice, clap four times, and then bow once more.

Clapping hands, a natural expression of pleasure or gratitude in daily life, is a respectful act to show sincere reverence to the enshrined *kami*.

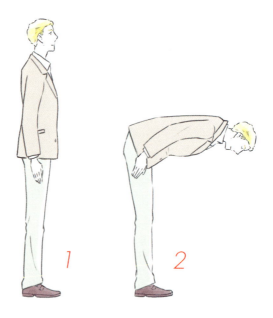

拝礼の作法

賽銭を入れ、鈴を鳴らしたら、柏手を打って拝礼する。この時の作法は、出雲大社(p.66)の「二拝四拍手一拝」のような例もあるが、明治時代以降に「二拝二拍手一拝」(1〜5)が定着していった。

拍手はコンサートやスピーチのみならず、日常生活のなかで喜びや嬉しさをあらわす時に自然に行われるもので、神社においても神を深く思う、敬愛の心のあらわれである。

How to Offer Tamagushi

On some special occasions such as purifications and devotions, visitors offer a sprig of the sacred *sakaki* tree decorated with white paper strips called *tamagushi*, to pray. This ritual is called *tamagushi hairei*. When praying, visitors are encouraged to take a *tamagushi* in both hands (1, 2), turn it toward the *kami* (3, 4), then pray (5) and listen to the priest's prayer (6).

玉串の作法

お祓いや特別な祈願は拝殿内で行われる。この時、参拝者は神前に玉串を供えて祈願する。これを「玉串拝礼」という。玉串は右手を上にしてもち（1、2）、根元が神前に向かうように供え（3、4）、二拝二拍手一拝の作法でお参りする（5、6）。

Honden

The *honden* is the main shrine where the *kami* is enshrined and is the most sacred sanctuary. Shinto priests perform rituals there and offer food to the *kami* every day.

Inside the innermost room of the main shrine, where the *kami* resides, is a sacred object, the *goshintai*. It is often an object such as a mirror, a sword, a comma-shaped jewel (*magatama*, p. 108), a stone, a wooden statue or *gohei* (a wooden pole with *shide* paper). This sacred object is called *yorishiro*.

The enshrined *kami* is sometimes temporarily removed from the main shrine for a procession with a portable shrine, or during reconstruction works. At these times, the *kami* stays at a temporary shrine or a sacred ritual site. It should be noted that some *jinja* do not have a main shrine; for example, the *kami* of Omiwa Jinja Shrine is Mt. Miwayama (Sakurai, Nara), and that of Hiro Jinja Shrine is Nachi Waterfall (Nachikatsuura, Wakayama). The mountain and waterfall themselves are the sacred object where the *kami* reside.

本殿

本殿はその神社の祭神が鎮まる社殿で、もっとも神聖な場所である。神職によって日々、祭礼が行われ、神饌が捧げられている。

本殿の扉の奥には神座があり、そこには御神体が奉安されている。御神体は祭神の具体的な姿かたちそのものではない。神霊が宿るとされるもので、神霊は自然物や、御幣(木串に紙重という紙を取りつけたもの)、鏡などに依りつく。それを神の「依代」といい、ほかに剣・弓矢・勾玉(p. 108)・石・木像などがある。

祭神は常に本殿に鎮座しているわけではなく、社殿の修理や祭りの時には仮本殿や御旅所に遷座する。また、本殿のない神社もある。たとえば大神神社(奈良県桜井市)は三輪山を、飛瀧神社(和歌山県那智勝浦町)は那智の滝を御神体とする。

Representative types of ancient buildings are *shinmei-zukuri* of Ise Jingu Shrine (p. 64) and *taisha-zukuri* of Izumo Oyashiro Shrine (p. 66). The roof is gabled. The entrance set to the side of the roof that can be seen horizontally is called *shinmei-zukuri*, and the entrance is called *hirairi*. The entrance set to the side of the roof that can be seen as a triangle is *taisha-zukuri*, and the entrance is called *tsumairi*. Both floors are raised above the ground and have a handrail and veranda. On the roofline, a crossed wooden finial called *chigi* (p. 65①) and wooden bars arranged horizontally called *katsuogi* (p. 65②) are set.

Nagare-zukuri and *hachiman-zukuri* (p. 68) are derived from *shinmei-zukuri*, and *sumiyoshi-zukuri* and *kasuga-zukuri* are derived from *taisha-zukuri*. Some of the new types of buildings have neither *chigi* nor *katsuogi*.

古式の本殿の代表は、伊勢神宮の神明造(p. 64)と出雲大社の大社造(p. 66)である。どちらも開いた本を伏せたような切妻造の屋根だが、神明造の入り口は屋根が平面に見える側につき、大社造は屋根が三角に見える側につく。前者の入り口を平入、後者を妻入という。いずれも高床式で高欄をめぐらし、妻側の屋根の上に千木(p. 65①)という交差する2本の木を伸ばし、棟の上に鰹木(p. 65②)という横木を平行に並べている。

神明造からは、流造、八幡造(p. 68)などが派生し、大社造の流れを汲むものとしては住吉造、春日造などがある。新しい形式では、千木や鰹木がないものも多い。

Ofuda and Omamori

There is an office in the *jinja* precinct called *juyosho* where visitors can purchase amulets, talismans, and votive tablets. All amulets are properly purified so they can be distinguished from ordinary merchandise (*hatsuhoryo*, p. 108).

Ofuda (a tablet-type amulet made of wood or paper) is a sacred object in which divine spirits of the enshrined *kami* reside. The name of the *kami* or sacred words and pictures expressing divine energy are depicted on them. *Ofuda* should be placed on a

御札と御守

　神社には御札や御守、絵馬などをいただく場所がある。この場所を「授与所」という。並んでいるものは商品ではなく、神社がお祓いをして清めた授与品である。売買ではないので「買う」などの語はふさわしくない。謝礼は初穂料（p. 108）という。
　御札は神霊の宿った御霊代とされる。神札などともいい、祭神の名や霊力をあらわす文字や画像が描かれている。自宅の神棚に祀って家内安全・無病息災などを祈るが、

household altar or the upper part of a pillar.

Omamori are a smaller type of *ofuda* amulet that people can carry with them in a bag or wallet. Each *jinja* has various amulets for benefits such as safe childbirth, business prosperity, passing examinations, safety on the roadways, etc. Amulets are supposed to be repurchased every year, and old ones returned to their original place of purchase or neighborhood *jinja*.

神棚がなければ、柱などの高い位置に貼って祀る。
　御守は神符などともいい、御札の小型化したもので、身につけて神の守護を願う。どの神社にも安産祈願、商売繁昌、合格祈願、交通安全など多種類の御守がある。御札も御守も毎年新たにし、昨年のものは授与された神社に慎んで返納する。もし行けない場合は、近くの神社でもよい。

Omikuji

Omikuji are paper fortunes used for a type of divination or fortunetelling, said to have begun around the 13th century. A person shakes a box of sticks to mix them up, pulls one out at random, reads the number on it, and then receives the divination paper corresponding to that number, which tells their fortune. If the *omikuji* is tied to the branch of a tree its strenght is weakened. Therefore the wisdom is to tie a *omikuji* on the designated area of the shrine or take a *omikuji* back home.

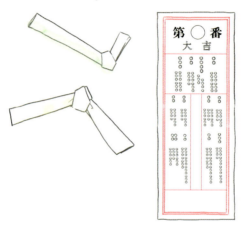

おみくじ

　おみくじは物事の裁定や個人の吉凶を判断する占いの一種で、その起源は1200年ごろという。筒状の箱を振って穴からみくじ棒を取り出し、そこに記された番号と同じ番号のみくじ箋（せん）を受け取る。箋には吉凶と運勢が記されている。おみくじを境内の木の枝に結ぶと樹勢をそぐことがあるので、神社指定の場所に結ぶか、自宅に持ち帰る。

Ema

Ema are votive tablets, and are offered to *jinja* to express gratitude or wishes. In old times, a living horse was offered as a gift to a *kami*, but over the course of time it was replaced by a wooden plaque with the picture of a horse. Nowadays, it is customary to hang the *ema* with handwritten prayers and wishes in a designated area. Shape is not fixed, and differs by *jinja*. For example, the leaf-shaped *ema* at Tsurugaoka Hachimangu Shrine (Kamakura, Kanagawa) is designed after the divine gingko tree.

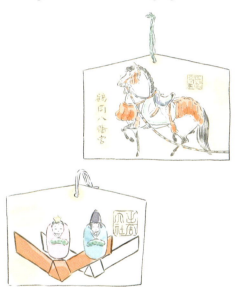

絵馬

　絵馬は祈願や祈願がかなったお礼のため、神社に奉納する額の一種である。昔は生きた馬を奉納していたが、その代用として板絵の馬が使われるようになったためこの名がある。現在では、余白や裏面に祈願の内容などを書き、絵馬掛けにつるす。形は定まったものでなく、神社ごとに異なる。鶴岡八幡宮（神奈川県鎌倉市）の絵馬には御神木であるイチョウの葉の形のものもある。

縁起物

　縁起物は、それを頒布する神社になんらかの由縁をもつもので、初詣 (p. 103) や神社の縁日 (p. 109) で授与され、飾っておくと神の加護が得られるというもの。破魔矢、招き猫、熊手などがある。
　毎年11月の酉の市 (p. 109) には、各地の鷲 (大鳥) 神社に露店が建ち並び、七福神

Engimono

Engimono is a good luck charm that usually can be purchased at *hatsumoude* (p. 103) or *ennichi* (p. 109). The famous ones are *hamaya* (evil destroying arrow), *maneki-neko* (beckoning cat), and *kumade* (rake).

Every year in November, there are festivals called *Tori no Ichi* (p. 109) at Otori Jinja shrines, where many street stalls sell special decorated rakes called *engi kumade* (good luck rakes), which are believed to "rake in" fortune. *Kumade* is made of bamboo and is decorated with *koban* (old gold coins), Ebisu (one of the popular *Shichifukujin* deities) and *otafuku* (happy homely woman) masks.

Hamaya is also very popular at New Year. It is believed that this special arrow is imbued with divine power to destroy misfortune. It was derived from the arrow at Tsurugaoka Hachimangu Shrine in the 13th century. These good luck charms are supposed to be renewed every year.

の恵比須やお多福、小判などを飾りつけた「縁起熊手」が飛ぶように売れる。熊手は福を「かきこむ」という。

　正月に人気があるのが破魔矢。「魔を破る」力があるとされる。13世紀に鶴岡八幡宮に奉納された朱塗矢が始まりとされる。熊手や破魔矢は毎年、新しくしよう。

Goshuin

Collecting divine seals has recently become popular. A Shinto priest affixes a *goshuin*, "divine seal", to a piece of paper and writes the date. Although the cost is generally set at 300 to 500 yen, there are also shrines which do not designate a fixed price. In such a case, one is meant to offer according to their means. Some *jinja*

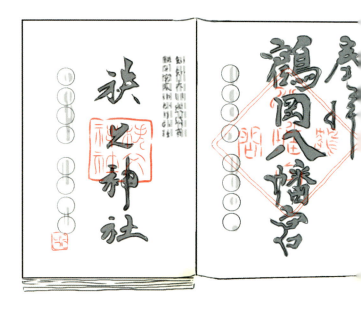

also provide the seals of auxiliary shrines.

A notebook for collecting such seals can be found at the amulet office, *juyosho*. It is usually designed by folding Japanese paper into multiple panels or attaching pages to a Japanese-style binding.

御朱印(ごしゅいん)

　近年は、社寺の御朱印集めがブームになっている。神社に参拝したしるしとして、神職が朱印帳に神社名の朱印を押し、参拝日などを墨書(はつびょう)する。初穂料は300円から500円ほどだが、金額を定めていない神社もあり、その場合はこちらの判断で応分の初穂料をお納めする。摂社や末社、兼務神社の御朱印をもらえる神社もある。

　朱印帳は厚めの表紙の屏風折(びょうぶおり)(折り本)や、和綴じ(わとじ)(和装本)が多い。あらかじめ神社の授与所などで求めることができる。

Sessha and Massha

In the precinct of the main shrine there are smaller shrines called *sessha* and *massha*.

Generally, *sessha* is an auxiliary shrine that is dedicated to *kami* closely related to the main shrine (*jinushigami*, p. 110), and *massha* is a more subordinate shrine that is dedicated to unrelated *kami*. Of course, the main shrine is the most important building, followed by *sessha*, and then by *massha*.

In auxiliary shrines, a special shrine, called *wakamiya*, is as important as the main shrine. *Wakamiya* generally enshrine a descendant or a prince of the *kami* that is enshrined in the main shrine. Both Kasuga Taisha Shrine (Nara) and Tsurugaoka Hachimangu Shrine have *wakamiya*.

摂社・末社

神社の境内には、本殿とは別に、小規模な社殿が祀られている。それが摂社と末社である。

一般に、摂社は、本殿に祀られる祭神の后神や御子神といったゆかりの深い神様や、その土地の地主神 (p. 110) を祀る神社で、末社はそれ以外の、ほかの神社から勧請した神様を祀る神社として区別される。格式はふつう、本社、摂社、末社の順とされる。

摂社のなかでも、若宮と呼ばれ、本社同様に重んじられているものがある。本社祭神の若君（御子神）の宮という意味である。春日大社（奈良市）や鶴岡八幡宮の若宮がそれで、春日大社の若宮にはさらに末社が付属している。

Chinju no Mori

A *jinja* is revered by each community or village, and is always surrounded by a thick forest, called *chinju no mori*. It is a typical landscape in the Japanese imagination. Parishioners gather at shrines and conduct ceremonies to pray for abundant harvest of rice and fish.

Mori is the Japanese word for "forest," and *jinja* used to be called *mori* in ancient times. In other words, *jinja* was essentially the same thing as a sacred forest where *kami* reside. For this reason, forests are treated as sanctuaries and, as such, their purity is maintained.

Moreover, *jinja* are usually located in an area with a headwater or at the foot of a mountain, rich with many precious plants and insects. The Japanese sense of home still seems to be preserved in these places.

鎮守の森

　日本では、村落ごとに住人がこぞって崇め敬う神社がある。これが鎮守である。鎮守の森はその神社をとりかこむ鬱蒼とした森のことで、多くの日本人の原風景となっている。村人は、鎮守の祭礼を共同で行うことで一体感をはぐくみ、神に豊作・豊漁を祈願し、感謝した。

　神社のことを古くは「もり」ともいっていた。つまり、神社とは本来、神の鎮まる神聖な森のことをいっていたのである。

　鎮守の森は山すそや水源地などにあり、かつてはその多くが禁足地とされてきた。そのため貴重な植物や昆虫などが今も生息している。鎮守の森には日本人の故郷へのイメージが残されている。

Shintaisan and Goshinboku

In Japanese classical writings, divine mountains where *kami* reside are called *shintaisan* or *kannabi*. Divine rocks are called *iwakura* or *iwasaka*, and divine trees are *goshinboku* or *himorogi*. The mountain itself, however, is not considered a *kami*. A *shintaisan* or *kannabi* is a mountain inhabited by *kami*. As such, it is considered taboo to enter a primeval forest surrounding a *shintaisan* and disturb its sacred residents. The original style of *jinja* began with a *torii* facing the depth of the forest, in line with the shrine buildings and *shintaisan*. This is the primary reason that shinto rituals are held at the foot of a mountain. In Nara, Omiwa Jinja Shrine is located at the foot of Mt. Miwayama, which is revered as a divine mountain, and ancient rituals were conducted there. Mt. Mikasayama at Kasuga Taisha Shrine is also a divine mountain.

A divine tree, *goshinboku,* is usually very old and large, and has a sacred straw rope, *shimenawa* (p. 110), tied around it making it easily noticeable. *Kami* reside in *goshinboku*, and such trees are diligently protected and cared for by *jinja*.

神体山・御神木

　神霊の鎮まる山のことを、古典では神奈備といい、岩であれば磐座・磐境、そして木であれば御神木・神籬という。一般に神体山は神奈備と同じ意味だが、山そのものが神ではない。神体山は神が降臨し、鎮座する山である。多くの場合、原生林におおわれ、入山することができない禁足地になっている。古い歴史をもつ神社の神域は、奥に向かって鳥居、社殿、神体山と並ぶことから、山麓祭祀が神社の主な起源とされる。奈良の大神神社は、神殿の背後の三輪山を神を祀るべき神聖な地とする古代祭祀を今に伝え、春日大社の御蓋山もまた、神体山である。

　御神木は樹齢何百年という巨木が多く、注連縄 (p. 110) がはられているのですぐわかる。神の依代であり、神社では大切に保護・管理している。

Chapter 2

Kannushi and Prayer

第二章

神職と祈り

Shinto Priest: Kannushi

A Shinto priest serves the *kami* of the shrine, and conducts ceremonies and other administrative tasks. Generally speaking, the priest is called *kannushi* or *shinkan* in Japanese, but there are some variations depending on the region and the historical period.

The *guji* is a chief priest who is in charge of festivities and administration. The next position is called *negi*, after which is *gonnegi*. A priest in training is called *shusshi*. Some *jinja* have a a vice priest position called *gonguji*.

Ise Jingu Shrine (p. 62) is an especially venerable *jinja* that enshrines the ancestral *kami* of the Japanese imperial family. Through its long history, Ise Jingu has come to have a special priest classification: the highest priest is called *saishu*, followed by *daiguji*, and *shoguji*.

Certain qualifications are required to become a *kannushi*, such as passing an examination administered by the Jinja Honcho (p. 111), and studying at academic institutions that have special *kannushi* training programs.

神職とは

神社で祀られている神に奉仕し、祭祀や運営をする仕事を神職といい、一般には神主、神官と呼ばれるが、時代、地域によってさまざまな呼び方がある。

神社の祭典、事務の最高責任者である宮司、その下に禰宜、権禰宜の職階があり、見習い職は出仕と呼ばれる。宮司の下に権宮司をおく神社もある。

伊勢神宮(p. 62)は皇室の祖先神を祀る特別な由緒のある神社で、その長い歴史のなかで、一般の神社と職制も異なり、最高位を祭主といい、次いで大宮司、少宮司と続く。

神職になるには資格が必要で、神社本庁(p. 111)傘下の神社に関しては、神社本庁の試験に合格するか、神職養成機関をもつ大学などで学習しなくてはならない。

Clothing of Kannushi

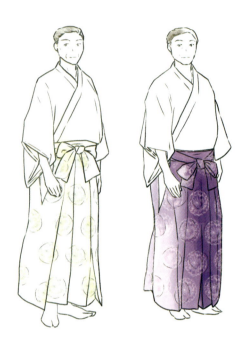

The outfits *kannushi* wear for ceremonies were derived from aristocratic dress of the Heian period. Depending on the type of ritual and the priest's position, clothes vary from simple to luxurious. *Kannushi* wear a hat called *kanmuri* or *eboshi* and hold

神職の服装
　神職が祭典の時に身につける服装は、平安時代の貴族の装束が起源である。祭典の種類と身分によって身につける装束が異なる。たとえば袴は身分によってイラストのように異なっている。

a wooden board in the right hand to express solemnity (p. 54). They also wear lacquered shoes called *asagutsu* made from the wood of the paulownia tree.

祭典の時、神職は冠や烏帽子と呼ばれるものを頭にかぶり、右手には笏といういかめしさを表現する木の持ち物を持つ (p. 54)。また神職の履物を浅沓といい、桐でつくったものに和紙を貼り、漆を塗ったものである。

Miko

Miko are shrine maidens, not priests, thus no qualifications are required. *Miko* are unmarried and directly employed by shrines. Their main duty is to perform a sacred dance during ceremonies and assist the priests. They wear a white inner kimono and red pleated *hakama* pantaloons. Their long hair is tied back with *mizuhiki* strings (p. 111). For ceremonies, they wear *chihaya*, a light white robe. Their appearance of purity and beauty comforts visitors.

In ancient times, *miko* were religious conduits who were believed to possess an ability to deliver divine words from *kami*. Based on Japanese myths and the traditions of Ise Jingu Shrine, it is evident that *miko* played an extremely important role in ancient religious rituals.

巫女

巫女は神職ではなく、特別な資格は必要ではない。神社ごとに採用され、神職を補佐している未婚の女性である。巫女は長い髪を水引(p. 111)などで結び、白衣に緋袴を着用する。巫女舞など神事に奉仕する時には、薄い白地の「千早」を羽織る。巫女の清楚で美しい姿は、神社に安らぎを添える。

古代社会においては、巫女は司祭者として、神の言葉を人々に宣託する力をもっていた。日本神話や伊勢神宮の古い制度をみれば、古代の神祭りに女性が極めて重要な役割を担っていることがわかる。

Norito

Norito are formal prayers a *kannushi* recites for *kami* in rituals. *Norito* are only recited by a chief priest, while envoys sent from the Jinja Honcho recite liturgies called *saishi*. Invocations from worshipers are called *kiganshi*. These prayers convey the significance of a ceremony as well as reverence toward divine virtue through sincerity and vows to accomplish one's endeavors.

Since ancient times, there has been a belief in *kotodama,* the power of language. Words themselves are believed to possess spirituality. Thus, when words are uttered, their meaning and content is materialized. It can therefore be said that the recitation of *norito* derives from a belief in *kotodama*.

祝詞

　一般に祝詞とは神祭りにおいて、神に対して申し上げる言葉のことをいう。神社の祭典における祝詞は宮司が申し上げるもので、祭詞は神社本庁からの使者が、祈願詞は崇敬者が申し上げるものである。こうした祝詞、祭詞、祈願詞は祭典の意義を明らかにすると同時に、神の威光を敬い、神の徳を称えて感謝の真心を捧げ、神の加護を祈り、みずからの努力を誓おうとするものである。

　日本の古い信仰の一つに言霊信仰というものがある。言葉そのものに霊力があり、その力が働いて言葉通りの事象が成就されると信じられたもので、祝詞はそうした信仰を継承するものである。

Shinsen

Shinsen is an offering of food for *kami* and serves an important ritual role. A *kami* is welcomed with the offering, and the offering itself is shared by worshipers after the ceremony. This is called *naorai*. The relationship between *kami* and worshipers is deepened when they share the food, and worshipers hope it will lead to greater blessings from the *kami*.

Shinsen is normally comprised of rice, *sake*, rice cakes, salt, water, seafood, seaweed, vegetables, fruits and sweets. Sometimes, seasonal fruits and vegetables or regional specialties are added. The list of *shinsen* reflects the traditional food culture of Japan. *Kannushi* bow to *shinsen* to pay respect, or sometimes wear a mask so as not to breathe on it. These special acts reveal the great respect with which *shinsen* is treated and how revered it is.

神饌

　神饌とは、神に供える食事のことで、祭典のなかで重要な位置を占める。神饌を捧げることで神迎えをし、そのお下がりを参列者たちがいただく。これを直会という。神が召し上がったものを人がいただくことで、神との結びつきが強くなり、その御加護も大いに期待できる。

　お供えする品目は、一般に米、酒、餅、塩、水、昆布などの海の幸、山の幸、野菜、菓子などで、これに旬の産物や地元の特産品が捧げられる。神饌の品目には、日本の食文化が反映されている。神前に供えるにあたり、神饌の一つ一つに敬意をあらわして頭を下げたり、神社によっては神前に供える時に息がかからぬよう覆面を用いたりしており、神饌がいかに重要に取り扱われているかがわかる。

Chapter 3

Kami and Jinja

第三章

神様と神社

Kami and Goshintoku

Japan is blessed with rich nature, and since ancient times, people have lived in close harmony with it. The ancient Japanese felt the divinity of nature in daily tasks such as agriculture, fishing, and hunting, and they revered the different aspects of it as *kami*. Before long, these revered *kami* became guardians of each community and clan. Therefore, it can be said that the number of *kami* is proportional to the number of natural phenomena and the diversity of people's daily lives.

These *kami* descended from heaven and resided in divine objects such as *shintaisan* (p. 45), and later were enshrined at *jinja*. Every *kami* is endowed with special powers to bless any wish. Especially revered throughout Japan were extraordinary *kami*, such as the *kami* of the sun which gives everything, the *kami* preventing epidemics, and the *kami* for safety at sea. Their divine virtue is called *goshintoku*.

Specific *kami* came to be revered during different historical eras and in different regions. During the age of the samurai, the guardian *kami* of samurai was worshipped, as well as the *kami* of prosperity who became popular in commercial districts. Visitors from all over Japan prayed at their *jinja*. Local branches of main *jinja* were also constructed throughout Japan and *kami* were re-

祭神と御神徳

　日本は古代から豊かな自然に恵まれ、人々はそのような自然とともに生きてきた。農業や漁労、狩猟など、日々の生活を支える自然の姿に霊力を感じ、それを神として崇めたのである。したがって、自然のさまざまな現象や人々の種々の生活によって、日本の神々はその数だけいるといってよい。

　これらの神々は、全国各地の神体山(p. 45)などに依りつき、鎮座した。この神々を祭神として祀るのが神社である。どの神も一様に諸願をかなえる力をもつが、とりわけ太陽のように万物をはぐくむ力をあらわす神、荒ぶる力で疫病を治める神、航海の安全に力を発揮する神などがいる。その特別な力を御神徳という。

　時代や地域によって、人々の信仰を集める神は異なり、武士の世では武威をあらわす

enshrined in them. Even though there are numerous *kami* and *jinja*, the chief *kami* of the Shinto pantheon is Amaterasu Omikami who is enshrined in Ise Jingu. Several important *jinja* in Japan, including Ise Jingu, are introduced from the next page.

Matsuri

Matsuri are events at which individuals and groups honor and worship their personal *kami*. They can also be called *sarei* or *saishi*, words that both mean festival, but have religious connotations. Shinto ritual prayers serve as an integral part of religious festivals wherein participants express faith in the *kami* and give praise to their *goshintoku*. Religious observances are followed by a celebration to show gratitude to *kami*. Most types of *matsuri* are associated with traditional food, dress and music.

神が、商業が盛んな所では商売繁昌の神が求められ、全国から多くの参拝客が押し寄せるか、あるいは神霊そのものが各地に分祀されていった。そうした神々の中心になるのが天照大御神。この天照大御神を祀る伊勢神宮をはじめとして、日本各地の有力な神社をこの章で紹介する。

祭り

個人であれ、集団であれ、みずからの崇め敬う神に対して行うのが祭りで、祭礼、祭祀ともいう。祭りの儀礼を通じて神は御神徳を増し、人は神威を享受する。祭りは神に祈り、奉仕することであり、神社で日々行われる神事も祭りである。

Ise Jingu
(Ise, Mie)

Ise Jingu is known as the spiritual home of Japan and is located amid the beautiful nature of Shima Peninsula. It is the holiest and most important Shinto shrine among all others, and is officially called Jingu.

Jingu is divided into two different shrines: Kotaijingu, or Naiku, dedicated to Amaterasu Omikami, the ancestral *kami* of the imperial family, and Toyouke Daijingu, or Geku, dedicated to Toyouke no Omikami, the provider of sacred food. Toyouke no Omikami was invited to Geku through the divination of Amaterasu Omikami. It is customary for worshipers to visit Geku first and then Naiku, which is five kilometers away.

Naiku Shrine was founded about 2,000 years ago, and Geku Shrine was established 500 years later. *Goshoden*, the main shrines, are rebuilt every 20 years to revive their divine energy. This ceremony is called *Shikinen Sengu*.

伊勢神宮（三重県伊勢市）

伊勢神宮は「日本人の心のふるさと」といわれ、山海の自然が美しい伊勢湾に面する志摩半島に鎮座する。すべての神社の上に立つ特別な存在である。伊勢神宮の正式名称は「神宮」である。

神宮には、皇室の祖先神とされる天照大御神を祀る皇大神宮（通称・内宮）と、天照大御神の食事を司る豊受大御神を祀る豊受大神宮（通称・外宮）がある。豊受大御神は天照大御神の神託によって招かれた神である。

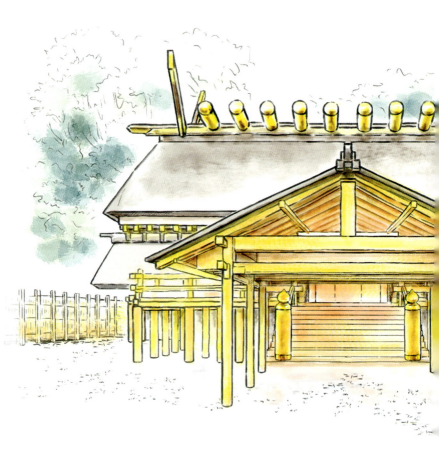

Naiku

Enshrined *kami*:
Amaterasu Omikami, a female *kami* symbolizing the sun. She lights up the universe and is the mother of life.
Goshintoku: *kami* of the sun
Shinshi: hen

Geku

Enshrined *kami*:
Toyouke no Omikami
Goshintoku: abundant harvests

① *chigi*   ② *katsuogi*

　今から2000年ほど前に内宮(左図)ができ、その約500年後に外宮が創建された。どちらも御正殿(神宮では本殿をこう呼ぶ)は神威を再生させるため、20年ごとに建て替えられる。これを「式年遷宮」という。
　内宮と外宮は5kmほど離れており、先に外宮をお参りし、それから内宮にお参りするのが正式な参拝の作法とされる。
内宮【祭神】天照大御神【御神徳】太陽の神
外宮【祭神】豊受大御神【御神徳】五穀豊穣
【神使】鶏

Izumo Oyashiro

(Izumo, Shimane)

The Izumo region is known as an important site of Japanese mythology. Izumo Oyashiro is dedicated to Okuninushi no Okami who handed over the land to Amaterasu Omikami after completing the earthly world. Izumo Oyashiro was given to Okuninushi no Okami in exchange for bringing the earthly world to completion. The height of the main building was about 48 meters in the Heian period, and huge pillars have been excavated in the precinct.

Every year in October of the old calendar (November), a famous festival called Kamiari Sai is held, and it is believed that all the *kami* in Japan gather at Izumo. Also, Izumo Oyashiro has the largest sacred straw rope, or *shimenawa* (p. 110). It is 13 meters long, 8 meters thick, and weighs 4.5 tons.

Enshrined *kami*: Okuninushi no Okami
Goshintoku: finding a good relationship or marital ties

出雲大社（島根県出雲市）

出雲地方は神話の舞台として知られる。出雲大社は、大国主大神が完成させた地上の国を、天上界の支配神・天照大御神に譲るかわりに造営してもらったのが創祀と伝える。平安時代の本殿は約48mの高さがあったとされ、これを推定させる大きな柱が境内から出土している。

毎年、旧暦10月（新暦で11月ごろ）には、日本全国の神々が出雲につどうとされ、「神在祭」が盛大に挙行される。神楽殿の注連縄（p. 110）は長さ13m、太さ8m、重さ約4.5tで日本最大級の大きさである。

【祭神】大国主大神　【御神徳】縁結び

Hachiman Jinja

There are about 40,000 branches of the Hachiman Jinja throughout Japan. It is also called Hachimangu or Hachimansha. The head Hachiman Jinja is Usa Jingu (Usa, Oita), founded in 571. In the Heian period (8th-12th century), Iwashimizu Hachimangu (Yawata, Kyoto) was enshrined as the guardian *kami* of the capital, Kyoto. Following the establishment of the Kamakura shogunate by Yoritomo Minamoto (p. 112), the *kami* of Hachiman was enshrined in Kamakura as the guardian *kami*. This marks the foundation of Tsurugaoka Hachimangu (Kamakura, Kanagawa).

Also enshrined in Hachiman Jinja is Emperor Ojin, the fifteenth emperor, who was born while his mother Empress Jingu was leading a battle. He is known as the *kami* for military protection and safe childbirth.

Enshrined *kami*: Emperor Ojin, Empress Jingu, Himegami
Goshintoku: protecting the nation, avoiding misfortune, guardian *kami* of samurai
Shinshi: pigeon

八幡神社

八幡神社は全国に約4万社ある。八幡宮や八幡社と呼ばれることも多い。総本社は九州の宇佐神宮(大分県宇佐市)で、571年の創祀。9世紀半ばに京の都の守護神として勧請され、石清水八幡宮(京都府八幡市)が創建された。源頼朝(p. 112)が鎌倉幕府を開くと、今度は、幕府の守護神として鎌倉に勧請された。これが鶴岡八幡宮(神奈川県鎌倉市)である。

応神天皇は第15代天皇。八幡大神はその御神霊である。応神天皇は、母・神功皇后がみずから陣頭指揮をして進軍中に誕生したことから武神として知られ、また安産の神としての信仰もある。

【祭神】応神天皇、神功皇后、比売神　【御神徳】国家鎮護、厄除、武神　【神使】鳩

Inari Jinja

The head Inari Jinja is Fushimi Inari Taisha (Kyoto), founded in 711. There are about 30,000 branches of Inari Jinja throughout Japan; this number rises to over a million if personal household shrines are included. It has the highest number of branches in Japan.

Although it is famous for its 1,000 vermilion-colored *torii*, a *shintaisan* must be noted behind it, Mt. Inariyama Mitsugamine. This is where the *kami* of Inari descended and rice was first cultivated. On the lunar calendar's first day of the horse in February, a renowned festival called Hatsu Uma Taisai is held. Visitors make a pilgrimage to Mt. Inariyama Mitsugamine to commemorate the day the *kami* of Inari first appeared.

Uka no Mitama no Okami is the main Inari *kami*. *Uka* originally referred to "food." In the Edo period (17th-19th century), Inari became widely recognized as the *kami* of prosperity, especially in business.

Enshrined *kami*: Uka no Mitama no Okami
Goshintoku: abundant harvests, prosperity in business
Shinshi: fox

稲荷神社

　稲荷神社は全国に約3万社あり、個人の屋敷神まで数えると100万を超えるともいわれ、日本最多の神社である。

　総本社は伏見稲荷大社(京都市)で、創祀は711年。朱塗りの千本鳥居が有名だが、くぐり抜けた先に「お山」(稲荷山三ケ峰)があり、そこに稲荷神が降臨し、稲が生じたという聖地である。有名な「初午大祭」(2月初午の日)は、稲荷神の降臨した日に行われるお祭りで、お山をめぐる多くの参詣者でにぎわう。

　宇迦之御魂大神の「ウカ」という語は、古くは食べ物のことを意味する。江戸時代に諸業繁栄の神、とりわけ商売繁昌の神として信仰を集めるようになった。

【祭神】宇迦之御魂大神　【御神徳】五穀豊穣、商売繁昌　【神使】狐

Aoi Matsuri
葵祭

Kamo Jinja

Kamo Jinja enshrines the guardian *kami* of the Kamo clan who governed Kyoto before the relocation of the capital from Nara in the 8th century. After the relocation, Kamo Jinja was worshiped as the home of the guardian *kami* of the new capital. There are about 300 branches of Kamo Jinja in Japan.

Every May, Kamo Matsuri is held by Kamo Wakeikazuchi Jinja (commonly Kamigamo Jinja) and Kamo Mioya Jinja (Shimogamo Jinja) to pray for bountiful harvests. This festival features a procession of participants wearing imperial attire from the 9th-11th century. The pattern of two leaves from the *aoi* plant (hollyhock, p. 112) are printed or laced on the costumes, giving the event the name of Aoi Matsuri (p. 72-73). These are the two oldest shrines in Kyoto and are designated as World Heritage Sites. Most of the shrine's buildings are designated as National Treasures or Important Cultural Property of Japan, including the 36 buildings of Kamigamo Jinja and the 55 buildings of Shimogamo Jinja.

Enshrined *kami*:
Kamo Wakeikazuchi no Okami (Kamigamo Jinja)
Tamayorihime no Mikoto, Kamo Taketsunumi no Mikoto (Shimogamo Jinja)
Goshintoku: protecting the capital city

賀茂神社

祭神は都ができる前から京都を治めていた賀茂氏の氏神で、京都に都ができると王城鎮護の神となった。全国に約300の分社がある。

毎年5月、9〜11世紀の王朝の装束を着た行列が京都の町中を進む「賀茂祭」を行うのが、賀茂別雷神社(通称・上賀茂神社)と賀茂御祖神社(通称・下鴨神社)。全員がハート型の二葉葵(p. 112)の葉を身に飾るため、一般に「葵祭」(p. 72-73)と呼ばれ、五穀豊穣を祈願する祭りである。多くの社殿が国宝・重要文化財で、上賀茂神社では36棟、下鴨神社では55棟が指定されている。いずれも京都最古の神社で、世界遺産。

【祭神】賀茂別雷大神(上賀茂神社) 玉依媛命、賀茂建角身命(下鴨神社)
【御神徳】王城鎮護

Kasuga Jinja

The head Kasuga Jinja is Kasuga Taisha (Nara), and boasts about 3,000 branches throughout Japan. Kasuga Jinja enshrines the guardian *kami* of the Fujiwara clan (p. 113), who were highly distinguished aristocrats. However, the Fujiwara clan was also connected to the imperial family, so Kasuga Jinja was specifically venerated by the imperial court as a guardian *kami* for the capital.

Kasuga Taisha is located at the foot of Mt. Mikasayama, the famous divine mountain called *kannabi* in ancient Shintoism, meaning "where gods sit." It is also a designated World Heritage Site. In December, a festival called Kasuga Wakamiya Onmatsuri is held. The festival plays a very important role in Japanese art history and is known for featuring the best in Japanese traditional performing arts.

Enshrined *kami*: Takemikazuchi no Mikoto, Futsunushi no Mikoto, Ame no Koyane no Mikoto, Himegami
Goshintoku: protecting the capital city, guardian *kami* of samurai
Shinshi: deer

春日神社

総本社は春日大社(奈良市)で、全国に約3000の分社がある。祭神は、もともと名門貴族・藤原氏(p. 113)の守護神であったものだが、藤原氏が朝廷の外戚となっていたため朝廷から特別の崇敬を受け、京城守護の神ともなった。

春日大社は神奈備山として有名な御蓋山の麓に鎮座し、世界遺産。12月に行われる「春日若宮おん祭」は日本最高の芸能祭典といわれ、日本の芸能史を語るうえで、重要な祭りである。

【祭神】武甕槌命、経津主命、天児屋根命、比売神
【御神徳】京城守護、武神 【神使】鹿

Tenmangu

The enshrined *kami* of Tenmangu is Michizane Sugawara. Representative shrines are Dazaifu Tenmangu (Dazaifu, Fukuoka) and Kitano Tenmangu (Kyoto). There are about 12,000 branches of Tenmangu or Tenjinsha in Japan.

Michizane Sugawara (late 9th-10th century) was born into a distinguished scholarly family and later became a bureaucrat. Accused of political slander, he was confined to govern a marginal area in the Kyushu region and eventually died in despair while asserting his innocence. Dazaifu Tenmangu and Kitano Tenmangu were founded to comfort his spirit.

Enshrined *kami*: Michizane Sugawara
Goshintoku: successful study and scholarship
Shinshi: ox

天満宮

菅原道真を祭神として祀る神社で、天神社ともいう。代表的な神社として太宰府天満宮(福岡県太宰府市)と北野天満宮(京都市)がある。全国には約1万2000社の天満宮・天神社がある。

菅原道真は、9世紀半ばから10世紀にかけての人で、学問の名家に生まれた。官僚として朝廷で高位に昇進したが、政略によって讒言され、九州に左遷させられた。道真は身の潔白を訴えながら失意のうちに亡くなり、その霊を和ませるために建てられたのが太宰府天満宮と北野天満宮である。

【祭神】菅原道真　【御神徳】学問の神　【神使】牛

Kumano Jinja

Kumano is located in the southeast area of Wakayama prefecture, where three mountains called Kumano Sanzan are worshiped. It has been a sacred place since ancient times. There are more than 3,000 branches of Kumano Jinja in Japan.

Kumano Sanzan is a collective term for Kumano Hongu Taisha (Tanabe), Kumano Hayatama Taisha (Shingu), and Kumano Nachi Taisha (Nachikatsuura). Kumano Nachi Taisha is famous for its waterfall. The three shrines are located 20 to 40 kilometers away from each other and are connected by the Kumano Kodo (Kumano Pilgrimage Routes). The three shrines and routes have all been registered as World Heritage Sites.

Enshrined *kami*:
Ketsumiko no Okami (Kumano Hongu Taisha)
Kumano Hayatama no Okami (Kumano Hayatama Taisha)
Kumano Fusumi no Okami (Kumano Nachi Taisha)
Goshintoku: blessing for next life, recovery from illness, prosperity in general
Shinshi: *yatagarasu* (a mythical three-legged crow from ancient Japanese legend)

熊野神社

　和歌山県の南東部にある熊野は古代からの霊地で、そこにある熊野三山が信仰の対象である。全国に3000社以上の熊野神社がある。

　熊野三山とは、熊野本宮大社(田辺市)、熊野速玉大社(新宮市)、そして那智の滝がある熊野那智大社(那智勝浦町)を総称したもの。それぞれ20〜40km離れ、参詣の道「熊野古道」で結ばれている。神社・古道ともに世界遺産。

【祭神】家津御子大神(熊野本宮大社)　熊野速玉大神(熊野速玉大社)　熊野夫須美大神(熊野那智大社)
【御神徳】来世加護、病気平癒、現世利益　【神使】八咫烏

Otaue Shinji
御田植神事

協力／住吉大社

Sumiyoshi Jinja

The head Sumiyoshi Jinja is Sumiyoshi Taisha (Osaka). Enshrining the guardian *kami* of sea transportation, there are about 2,300 branches in Japan. The three *kami* of Sumiyoshi were born when Izanagi no Mikoto was purified at sea. These three *kami* led the fleet when Empress Jingu was crossing the ocean.

Sumiyoshi Taisha was founded in the early 3rd century. It's main shrine is a National Treasure and includes four main buildings. Three of them line up in a single line similar to the layout of a fleet of ships. Every year on June 14, the rice planting Otaue Shinji Ritual (p. 78-79) is held, and has been designated an Important Intangible Folk Cultural Property of Japan. It is said that the festival originates from Empress Jingu's invitation of a female rice planter from Nagato no kuni (presently Yamaguchi) to prepare a rice field.

Enshrined *kami*: Sokotsutsu no Ono Mikoto, Nakatsutsu no Ono Mikoto, Uwatsutsu no Ono Mikoto, Empress Jingu
Goshintoku: safety at sea, purification

住吉神社

総本社は住吉大社(大阪市)。海上交通の守護神で、全国に約2300の分社がある。伊弉諾尊が身についた穢れを祓うために海に入った時に生まれたのが住吉三神で、神功皇后の渡海に際し、船団を導いたとされる。

住吉大社の創祀は3世紀初め。本殿(国宝)は、4棟のうち3棟が縦一列に並び、船団を思わせる配置である。毎年6月14日に行われる「御田植神事」(p. 78-79)は国の重要無形民俗文化財。神功皇后が田を設け、長門国(山口県)から植女を召した故事に始まるという。

【祭神】底筒男命、中筒男命、表筒男命、神功皇后
【御神徳】航海安全、祓の神

Gionsha

The head Gionsha is Yasaka Jinja (Kyoto), a World Heritage Site, where a famous festival called Gion Matsuri is held. The 2,300 branches of Gionsha conduct similar festivals each summer.

The enshrined *kami*, Gozu Tenno, is not an indigenous Japanese *kami* but a deity originally from India via China, who prevented epidemics. Gionsha was founded in the middle of the 7th century, and Gozu Tenno was syncretized with Susano no Mikoto, a *kami* derived from Japanese mythology.

Gion Matsuri began in the mid-9th century to eradicate and prevent the epidemics that started to proliferate. Since then, Gion Matsuri livens Kyoto every summer for an entire month from July 1st.

Enshrined *kami*: Susano no Mikoto (Gozu Tenno)
Goshintoku: preventing epidemics

祇園社

総本社は八坂神社(京都市)で、有名な祇園祭を行う神社である。7世紀半ばに創建されたとも伝えられ、全国に約2300の分社があり、そこでも少なからず祇園祭が行われている。祇園社の祭神である牛頭天王は、本来日本の神でなく、インドの神であったものが中国を経て日本に伝来した。病疫を防ぐ神として牛頭天王の信仰が受け入れられ、牛頭天王は日本神話の素戔嗚尊に習合されていった。

祇園祭は、日本を代表する祭りの一つで世界遺産。疫病が大流行した9世紀半ば、疫病退散を祈って行われたのが始まりで、7月1日から1か月間、真夏の京都を熱狂につつむ。

【祭神】素戔嗚尊(牛頭天王) 【御神徳】疫病退散

Sengen Jinja

Sengen Jinja is a shrine that honors Mt. Fuji—one of the most representative symbols of Japan—as a *shintaisan*. Mt. Fuji has been revered for thousands of years for both its beautiful shape and the belief that it is a place where *kami* reside. The head of Sengen Jinja is Fujisan Hongu Sengen Taisha (Fujinomiya, Shizuoka), which is designated as a World Heritage Site. The shrine buildings were first constructed at the present site in the early 9th century, but its history preceding the buildings is much older. There are about 1,300 branches of Sengen Jinja throughout Japan.

Mt. Fuji was also revered as a *kami* of fire because of its frequent eruptions. The spling melt from Mt. Fuji has produced many natural springs, so it is also worshiped as a *kami* of water and harvest.

Enshrined *kami*: Konohana no Sakuyahime no Mikoto
Goshintoku: preventing fire, protecting springs, safe childbirth

浅間神社

日本を代表する山・富士山を神体山として祀る神社。富士山はその美しい姿とともに神の宿る山として古くから信仰を集めている。世界遺産の富士山本宮浅間大社（静岡県富士宮市）を中心に、全国に約1300の浅間神社がある。浅間大社の社殿が現在地に建立されたのは9世紀初めだが、創祀はもっと古く、社殿はなかった。

富士山はたびたび噴火したため、火の神としても畏れられ、崇められた。また、富士山の雪解け水は火山礫層にしみ込んで山麓に多くの湧水を出すことから、水と豊穣の神ともされている。

【祭神】木花之佐久夜毘売命　【御神徳】火難除、湧水守護、安産

Munakata and Itsukushima Jinja

Munakata Jinja enshrines three goddesses who descended to the earthly world from heaven by order of Amaterasu Omikami. The head shrine is Munakata Taisha (Munakata, Fukuoka) which consists of three major complexes: Hetsumiya on land, Nakatsumiya on the beach, and Okitsumiya on the isolated island of Okinoshima. At Okitsumiya, about 80,000 ancient ritualistic items were excavated, and it is clear that nationalistic rituals were conducted when Japan traded with the Korean Peninsula and mainland China. No women are allowed to land on Okinoshima, and only a *kannushi* of Munakata Taisha stays there regularly.

Itsukushima Jinja (Hatsukaichi, Hiroshima) is located on Miyajima Island and is registered as a World Heritage Site (p. 84). At the end of the 6th century, it was re-enshrined from Munakata Taisha. In the 12th century, the vermilion *torii* and shrine buildings were constructed in the sea. The main shrine is a National Treasure and was reconstructed in 1571 after sustaining damage from fire in battles.

Enshrined *kami*: Tagorihime no Kami, Tagitsuhime no Kami, Ichikishimahime no Kami
Goshintoku: safety at sea

宗像神社、厳島神社

宗像神社は宗像三女神を祀る神社で、全国に8500社以上ある。総本社は宗像大社(福岡県宗像市)。この三女神は天照大御神の命を受けて天上界から地上に降臨した。宗像大社は陸地にある辺津宮、海岸にある中津宮、孤島の沖ノ島にある沖津宮からなる。沖津宮では、かつて中国大陸や朝鮮半島との交流に伴う国家的祭祀が行われており、約8万点もの古代祭祀の品々が出土した。女人禁制の島で、宗像大社の神職のみが一人ずつ交代で常駐する。

厳島神社(広島県廿日市市)は、宮島に鎮座する世界遺産(左図)。6世紀の終わりに宗像大社から三女神を勧請して創建された。12世紀に海上に建つ朱の社殿と鳥居が造営されたが、戦火にあい、現在の本殿(国宝)は1571年の再建である。

【祭神】田心姫神、湍津姫神、市杵島姫神　【御神徳】海上交通守護

Toshogu

Toshogu enshrines Tokugawa Ieyasu (p. 113), the founder and first shogun of the Tokugawa Shogunate. The head of Toshogu Shrine is the World Heritage Site, Nikko Toshogu (Nikko, Tochigi), which has about 100 branches.

Tokugawa Ieyasu ended civil strife and other conflicts during the 16th century and formed a new stable social order that lasted for 260 years. This era was called the Edo period.

Nikko Toshogu was first constructed in 1617, the year after Ieyasu died. His grandson Iemitsu, the third shogun, rebuilt the shrine as it is now. The buildings of Toshogu are very famous for their marvelous colorful carvings. The Yomeimon gate at the entrance and *Nemuri Neko* (sleeping cat) carved by Jingoro Hidari are designated National Treasures and *Sanzaru* (three monkeys) is an Important Cultural Property of Japan.

Enshrined *kami*: Tokugawa Ieyasu
Goshintoku: prosperity of descendants, protection of the Kanto region

東照宮

東照宮は17世紀初めに武家政権を樹立した徳川家康（p. 113）を祀る神社。世界遺産の日光東照宮（栃木県日光市）は、全国に100社以上ある東照宮の総本社。

徳川家康は16世紀の間続いた内乱を終息させ、新しい秩序と組織を形成し、その後、約260年にわたって江戸時代といわれる安定政権の礎を築いた。

日光東照宮は家康没後の翌年、1617年に創建され、孫の3代将軍家光によって現在の社殿に建て替えられた。極彩色の彫刻群が有名で、入り口に建つ陽明門や左甚五郎の作と伝えられる「眠り猫」が国宝、「三猿」は重文である。

【祭神】徳川家康　【御神徳】子孫繁栄、関東守護

Meiji Jingu
(Shibuya, Tokyo)

Meiji Jingu was founded in 1920 and enshrines Emperor Meiji and his consort Empress Shoken. While Japan was modernizing, Emperor Meiji took the initiative in formulating the constitution, parliamentary government, educational system, and industrial development. Empress Shoken endeavored to establish and manage the Japanese Red Cross Society.

The precinct is about 700,000m², upon which Tokiwa Forest was planted thanks to the efforts of countless volunteer youth and donations of 100,000 trees from all over Japan. Today, the forest is resplendent with evergreen trees. Although the forest is in the middle of Tokyo, it is said that endangered species and even new varieties of insects can be discovered there. It is sometimes referred to as "The Miracle Forest."

Omotesando, a popular and fashionable street for the young, was named after the main approach to Meiji Jingu.

Enshrined *kami*: Emperor Meiji, Empress Shoken
Goshintoku: protecting nation, peace of citizens

明治神宮（東京都渋谷区）

　近代化への道を走りはじめた日本にあって、憲法の制定、議会の開設、教育制度の確立、産業の開発など、国家の先頭に立った明治天皇と、明治天皇の皇后で日本赤十字社の設立と経営などに尽力した昭憲皇太后を祀る。1920年創建。

　約70万㎡の境内は、そのほとんどが当時の青年たちの勤労奉仕によって整備されたもので、全国から奉納された約10万本の樹木によって神宮の森（常磐の森）がつくられた。現在では、広葉樹が生い茂り、日本新発見の昆虫や絶滅危惧種が生息するなど、大都会では他に例をみない「奇跡の森」になっている。

　若者でにぎわう表参道は、文字通り明治神宮の表参道である。

【祭神】明治天皇、昭憲皇太后　【御神徳】国家鎮護、国民安寧

Kanda Myojin

(Chiyoda, Tokyo)

Kanda Jinja was founded in the early 8th century and is generally referred to as Kanda Myojin. Its roots are in the history of the Izumo clan who enshrined their ancestral *kami* when they pioneered and settled in a swampy area in the innermost part of Tokyo Bay. In the 10th century, General Masakado Taira was co-enshrined in Kanda Myojin. During his lifetime, he had rebelled against the imperial court in Kyoto for the independence of eastern Japan and was adored by the public in the Kanto region.

Kanda Myojin was prescribed as a guardian *kami* for the capital, Edo (presently Tokyo), by the second Tokugawa Shogun, Ietada. Since then, the Kanda Matsuri has been held, and every other year in May, a procession winds its way through Kanda, Otemachi, Nihonbashi, and Akihabara, accompanied by 200 large and small *mikoshi* (p. 115), enthusiastically transported by festival participants.

Enshrined *kami*: Onamuchi no Mikoto, Sukunahikona no Mikoto, Taira no Masakado no Mikoto
Goshintoku: guardian *kami* of the capital, Edo

神田明神（東京都千代田区）

　神田神社は8世紀初めの創建、一般には「神田明神」と呼ばれる。東京湾最奥部の低湿地に開拓入植した出雲（島根県）の氏族が、祖神大己貴命を祀ったことに始まる。
　その後、10世紀に京都の朝廷に対し、東日本の独立をめざして反乱を起こした武将・平将門を祀る。関東の民衆は将門を英雄として慕いつづけ、崇めたのである。
　神田神社は、江戸時代になり、2代将軍・徳川秀忠によって江戸総鎮守と定められる。「神田祭」はそのころから続く祭りである。1年おきの5月に神幸祭が行われ、神田、大手町、日本橋から秋葉原を大小200基の神輿（p. 115）が巡行する。
【祭神】大己貴命、少彦名命、平将門命　【御神徳】江戸総鎮守

Chapter 4

Rites of Passage

第四章

通過儀礼

Rites of Passage

At *jinja*, various rites of passages are conducted to pray for blessings and to avoid misfortune. These rites begin before a baby is born and continue through old age.

Obi-iwai

During the fifth month of pregnancy, an expectant mother goes through a sash-binding ritual in which a maternity belt is tied around her waist. This is a celebration called *obi-iwai*, and it includes prayers for a stable pregnancy and a safe birth. It is often held on the day of the dog according to the old Japanese calendar, because dogs can deliver many offspring with relative ease. It is also customary to share steamed rice and red beans (*sekihan*, p. 114) with the family and relatives after the ritual. Many *jinja* provide a maternity belt for expectant mothers, but some ask them to bring their own.

通過儀礼

神社では、人生の節目節目に厄災を祓い、神の加護を願う儀式が行われている。それは、まだ胎児の時から始まり、老境に至るまで続く。順に紹介しよう。

帯祝い

妊娠5か月目の戌の日に、妊婦が腹帯（岩田帯）をしめる儀式がある。これを「帯祝い」という。妊娠の安定期に入って、無事に出産を迎えるための儀式である。十二支の戌の日に行うのは、犬のお産が軽いのにあやかって安産を願うためである。お祓いをうけたあと、赤飯（p. 114）を炊き、親族とお祝いの食事をする風習もある。多くの神社では、お祓いをすませた腹帯を授与してくれるが、腹帯を持参するように指示される場合もある。

Hatsumiyamoude

A newborn baby's first visit to a local shrine (*ujigami*, p. 114) is called *hatsumiyamoude* (p. 94). It is a ritual whose aim is to pay deep appreciation to *kami* for the birth of the baby and pray for its continued growth.

Traditionally, the visit was made on the thirty-first or thirty-second day after the birth of a boy, and the thirty-second or thirty-third day after the birth of a girl. Nowadays, the day of a visit is determined based on practical matters, such as the physical condition of the mother and baby, and grandparents often accompany the baby and its parents.

For *hatsumiyamoude*, a newborn baby wears a beautiful white silk kimono with a celebration robe.

初宮詣（お宮参り）

初宮詣（p. 94）は、赤ちゃんが誕生後初めて、自分が住む土地の神様である氏神（p. 114）に参拝する行事である。無事に誕生したことのお礼と、これからの成長の加護を神様に祈願する。

お参りの時期は、古くからの風習で、男児は生後31日目か32日目、女児は生後32日目か33日目とされてきたが、最近では、母子の体調や天候も考えて日にちを決めるようになっている。両親のほか、祖父母が付き添うことも多い。

お宮参りの赤ちゃんには白羽二重（上質の白い絹布）の着物を着せ、紋付の祝い着を羽織らせる。

Hatsumiyamoude
初宮詣

Shichigosan
七五三

Shichigosan

Shichigosan (p. 95) is a celebration held on November 15 for boys aged three and five and girls aged three and seven to pray for their safety and a healthy future. There used to be a method of determining age called *kazoedoshi* (p. 114), but nowadays the actual age of children is widely prevalent. Weekends and national holidays in November are often preferred for visiting *jinja*.

This custom was derived from a ritual of the imperial court. The celebration for three-year-old boys and girls is called *kamioki*. The celebration for five-year-old boys is called *hakamagi* and for seven-year-old girls, *obitoki*.

On this celebration, *chitose-ame* (thousand-year candy) is given to children with prayers for long life. This candy first appeared in the Edo period (17th-19th century) and comes in long red and white sticks.

七五三

七五三(p. 95)は、男児が3歳と5歳、女児が3歳と7歳になった時に、その成長を祝う行事。11月15日、子供に晴れ着を着せて神社に参拝し、子供の成長を感謝し、これからの成長の加護を祈る。以前は数え年(p. 114)で行ったが、現在では満年齢で行うところもある。日にちも11月中のいずれかの土・日曜、祝日に行われることが多い。

昔は宮中の行事で、男女3歳の「髪置き」、男児5歳の「袴着」、女児7歳の「帯解き」という儀式があった。七五三はその名残である。

七五三には千歳飴がつきものだが、これは江戸時代に考案されたもの。紅白の長い飴に、子供の長寿を願う祈りがこめられている。

Seijinsai

This is a ritual recognizing that a youth has entered adult society. Today, the second Monday in January is a national holiday and local authorities host ceremonies for young people.

This custom has a long history, and was traditionally called *genpuku* for men and *mogi* for women. Although the ages of those participating in *genpuku* or *mogi* has varied over time, it has generally stayed between 12 and 16 years old.

At *jinja*, young men and women vow to fulfill their obligations as adults to *ujigami* and pray for blessings.

成人祭

成人式は、子供が大人社会の仲間入りすることを認めてもらう儀式で、現在では国民の祝日として1月の第2月曜日に定められ、主に地方公共団体主催の式典などが行われている。

成人を祝う儀式は古くからあり、男子では「元服」、女子では「裳着」といった。元服や裳着の年齢は時代によって異なるが、おおむね数え年で12 〜 16歳であった。

神社で行われる成人祭は、氏神に大人になったことを奉告し、神の祝福をうけ、社会人として責務を果たしていくことを誓うものである。

Kekkon-shiki

Kekkon-shiki means wedding ceremony in Japanese. The styles of weddings in Japan have always varied by region, and *kekkon-shiki* was recognized as a ritual focusing on the ceremony of marriage agreement.

Until the mid-20th century, *kekkon-shiki* was usually held at home, where the couple would exchange nuptial cups of *sake* symbolizing their commitment to one another. The first Shinto-style wedding was held in 1900 for the Crown Prince, Yoshihito at the shrine in the imperial court. Following this ceremony, Shinto weddings became the standard ceremony in Japan.

After World War II, the Japanese people faced many difficulties in daily life, and because it wasn't easy to host *kekkon-shiki* at home, Shinto weddings at *jinja* became popular throughout the country.

結婚式

日本の婚姻形態は、古くは著しい地域差があった。結婚式も婚姻成立式を中心とした儀礼を指し、儀式の内実もさまざまであった。

20世紀半ばまで、一般家庭においては結婚式は自宅で行われ、夫婦であることを約束する盃事が重要視された。現在見られるような神社の神様の前での結婚式は、1900年に大正天皇の結婚式が宮中の神前で行われたのが始まりという。

第2次世界大戦後の生活難のなかで、以前のように自宅であげる結婚式が難しくなり、そのため神社で行うことが普及していったのである。

Yakudoshi

Yakudoshi (*yaku*, p. 115) means inauspicious ages, and during these years, it is thought that a person should be careful in their daily life. It is said that misfortune or troubles will happen more than usual during these unlucky ages. The unlucky years are called *hon-yaku*. According to *kazoedoshi*, they are believed to occur at the ages of 25, 42, and 61 years old for men and 19, 33, and 37 years old for women. The year before each unlucky age is called *mae-yaku*, and the one after it is called *ato-yaku*. Forty-two years old for men and thirty-three years old for women are also known as *tai-yaku*, the unluckiest ages of all. These unlucky ages are customarily regarded as turning points in life during which a person's circumstances can become turbulent or disrupted. The custom cultivates an attitude of forbearance when bad things happen.

A person in the midst of *yakudoshi* is advised to visit *jinja* and receive purification to ward off misfortune and other problems.

厄年

厄 (p. 115) 年は災難にあったり、病気になったりすることが多いので、気をつけるべきとされる年齢。男性は数え歳の25歳、42歳、61歳、女性は19歳、33歳、37歳で、その年を本厄、その前後の年を前厄、後厄という。そのうち、男性の42歳と女性の33歳は大厄とされている。古くからの日本の風習だが、肉体的にも調子を崩しやすい節目の年齢といえるので、身を慎もうという警戒心がこうした信仰を生んだ。

厄年の人は、その年のできるだけ早めに神社に出向いて厄除けのお祓いをしてもらい、凶事や災難を回避する。

Toshi-iwai

Rituals to celebrate longevity are called *toshi-iwai*. According to *kazoedoshi*, *toshi-iwai* include years 61 (*kanreki*), 70 (*koki*), 77 (*kiju*), 80 (*sanju*), 88 (*beiju*), 90 (*sotsuju*) and 99 (*hakuju*). At these ages, a person is advised to visit *jinja* to receive blessings for continuing a healthy life.

Families and relatives gather at this time in hopes that some of the longevity will rub off on them, share a feast and present a gift for the celebration. Recently, the actual age is more prevalent, and celebration rituals can be held on birthdays or Respect for the Aged Day, which is celebrated on the third Monday in September.

According to the old Japanese calendar, 60 years is considered one life cycle, so *kanreki* means being reborn as a baby. During this celebration, red-colored gifts are presented because the color red signifies a newborn baby. Presents are not designated for the other celebrated ages.

年祝い

長寿を祝う儀式を一般に「年祝い」という。その年は神社に参拝し、平穏な人生を感謝し、今後の厄災を祓い、さらなる延命長寿を祈る。数え年61歳の還暦、70歳の古稀、77歳の喜寿、80歳の傘寿、88歳の米寿、90歳の卒寿、99歳の白寿などがある。

家族や親類などが集まり、お祝いの食事をしたり、贈り物をしたりして周りの者も長寿にあやかる。最近では満年齢で祝うことも多く、誕生日のほか、敬老の日(9月第3月曜日)に行われることもある。

還暦は、生まれた年の干支に戻るため、「赤子に還る」という意味で赤色の品を贈るが、ほかの年祝いでは贈り物の決まりはない。

Hatsumoude

Hatsumoude refers to the first visit to *jinja* on New Year's day, and is traditionally done at one's *ujigami*. These days, visiting a famous *jinja* or large Buddhist temple has become popular. Visitors express gratitude for their good fortune during the past year, and pray for a healthy and peaceful life in the new year.

Reitaisai

The most important ceremony for *jinja* is called *reitaisai* or *reisai*. This ceremony is either deeply connected to the history of *jinja*, its foundation date, or the *kami* and is usually held only once a year, although some *jinja* conduct it twice in spring and autumn. Annual *reitaisai* include not only very solemn rituals, but also *togyo*, a procession accompanying *mikoshi* (p. 115). Various forms of entertainment, such as dancing, singing, *kagura* (p. 116), *yabusame* (p. 116), and *sumo* (p. 117) may also be performed to please the enshrined *kami*.

初詣
　初詣は、新年になり、初めて神社に参拝することで、自分の所の氏神へ詣でるというのが古い形である。現在では、著名な神社や寺に参拝に出かけることが多い。参拝者は拝殿の前に進み、旧年の無事を感謝し、新たな1年の平安を祈願する。

例大祭
　神社でもっとも重要な祭りを「例大祭」、または「例祭」という。神社の祭神や起源に密接な祭りで年に1回、その神社と神様にゆかりの深い日に行われるが、年に2回、春と秋に行う神社もある。おごそかな神事とともに、神輿 (p. 115) の渡御があり、また神様に奉納するさまざまな芸能や神楽 (p. 116)、流鏑馬 (p. 116)、相撲 (p. 117) などが行われる。

Appendix

Glossary

Matsuri Festivals to Visit

付録

用語集
訪ねてみたい祭り

Glossary | 用語集

Introduction

Nihon Shinwa

Japanese mythology embraces Shinto as well as agriculturally based folk religion. There are innumerable Japanese myths dealing with everything from the creation of the Japanese archipelago to the many gods and goddesses, the underworld, the stars and planets, as well as the origins of the imperial family. Japanese myths are based predominantly on *Kojiki*, *Nihon Shoki* and *Fudoki* which were written in the 8th century, in addition to complementary texts such as *Kogoshui*, written in the 9th century. According to Japanese mythology, Izanagi no Mikoto and Izanami no Mikoto created the land of Japan, and are parents of Amaterasu Omikami, the sun goddess.

はじめに

日本神話 にほんしんわ

　日本の神々の物語を記述したものに、8世紀にまとめられた『古事記』『日本書紀』や『風土記』、9世紀の『古語拾遺』といったものがある。これらに記されている神々の物語は氏族や地域社会によって語りつがれてきたもので、数多くの神々が登場する。そうした神々には、喜び、悲しみ、嘆き、争いといった極めて人間的な姿をあらわす神もいれば、自然そのものの神もいる。
　そのなかで伊弉諾尊・伊弉冉尊の二神は、日本の国土を生み出し、また、さまざまな自然界の神々を生んだ神である。皇室の祖先神とされる天照大御神は、この二神から生まれた。天照大御神は万物をはぐくむ太陽を象徴する神で、あらゆる神々のなかで最高位にあり、日本国民全体の総氏神である。

Chapter 1

Ichinomiya

A historical term referring to the Japanese Shinto shrines with the highest rank in a particular province or prefecture. *Ichinomiya* are part of the system of classification and ranking of shrines. The prefectural governor, dispatched by the imperial court of Kyoto, would worship at a shrine soon after arrival at his post, thereby lending prestige to particular shrines.

Kegare

The Japanese term for a state of pollution and defilement, important particularly in Shinto as a religious term. Typical causes of *kegare* are contact with any form of death, disease, blood or menstruation. This condition can be resolved through purification rites called *misogi*. *Kegare* can have an adverse impact not only on the person directly affected, but also on the community to which they belong.

第一章

一宮 いちのみや

10世紀ごろに成立したもので、全国の国ごとに一宮があった。その国で一番高い権威と格式をもつ神社で、京の朝廷から派遣された地方長官は、着任後、最初に参拝した。一宮は慣習的に定められたもので、時代によって一宮となる神社が変動することもあったが、その多くは現在でも有名な神社である。

穢れ けがれ

清浄であることを第一とする神道にあって、忌まれる不浄・不潔な状態。死を弔い、病気を見舞っても穢れがうつるとされ、浄化するためには禊ぎが必要である。穢れを運ぶ悪い気を邪気といい、心身の清浄をけがすものである。

Hiyoshi Jinja

One of the main Shinto schools with traditions traceable to early historical periods. Based on the cult of Sanno (the Mountain King), and the head shrine is Hiyoshi Taisha (Otsu, Shiga). This superlative shrine of *Sanno* Shintoism enshrines Oyamakui no Kami whose father is Otoshi no Kami, the farming god, and whose mother is Ameshirukaru Mizuhime, the water goddess.

Magatama

Comma-shaped beads made with precious stones such as agate and crystal as well as earthenware originally developed in ancient Japan. It is thought that people hung strings of these beads on their necks first as decorative jewelry, and later as religious objects for ceremonies to avoid evil spirits.

Hatsuhoryo

An additional fee customarily dedicated to *kami* when participating in ceremonies. *Hatsuho* were the first grains of rice of the year offered to *kami* as appreciation for the harvest, and money is used as a substitution.

日吉神社 ひよしじんじゃ

総本社は日吉大社（滋賀県大津市）。日吉山王社とも呼ばれ、大山咋神を祀る。父神は農耕神である大年神、母神は水神の天知迦流美豆比売であり、大山咋神はこの二つの性格を併せ持つといわれ、土木の知識に優れ、種々の開拓事業に尽くした。

勾玉 まがたま

古代日本で独自に発達した装身具で、主に瑪瑙・水晶といった貴石でつくられ、動物の牙や胎児のような形をしている。紐を通して首に下げ、魔除けにしたとされ、祭祀にも用いられた。

初穂料 はつほりょう

初穂はその年に初めて収穫されたお米のことで、神前に供えて感謝の意を表す。初穂料は、初穂の代わりに供える金銭のこと。玉串料は、玉串の代わりに供えるもので、

When people ask for a prayer in person, they pay *tamagushiryo*, a monetary substitute for the sacred *tamagushi* branch.

祈祷をお願いする際などに納める。

Ennichi

A day believed to have a special connection to a particular Japanese deity. In Japan, people commonly believe that visiting shrines on these auspicious days may bring greater fortune than on other days, and people regularly pray for health, good fortune and success in business. Festivals are naturally held to coincide with these special calendar days.

縁日 えんにち

神社の創建や祭神の降臨・降誕など、神社にゆかりの深い日。ふだんにまさる御利益が得られるとされ、地域の生活と深く関わっている。境内や参道には、参拝客を迎える多くの露店が出る。

Tori no Ichi

A fair held on the days of the rooster in November at various Otori Jinja shrines found across Japan. The deity of good fortune and successful business is enshrined at Otori Jinja shrines, and they attract many worshipers at festival time. There are several days of the rooster in November, and on these days, a fair is set up in the shrine precincts, with open-air stalls selling *kumade* rakes for "raking in" wealth and good fortune.

酉の市 とりのいち

各地の鷲神社で11月の酉の日に行われ、開運や商売繁昌などを祈願する祭りとともに境内で行われる市。11月中に2回か3回あり、「一の酉」「二の酉」などといい、「三の酉」の市がある年は火事が多いとされる。この市ではさまざまな縁起物をつけた熊手が売られる。熊手は福を招き寄せるものといわれ、商人をはじめ多くの人が買い求める。

Jinushigami / Jishushin

The Shinto folk deities of an area of land (the name literally means "land-master-god"). These *kami* are thought to have occupied the land long before people set foot there, so settlers established shrines to the local resident *kami* to gain their favor or blessing.

Shimenawa

Shimenawa are lengths of laid rice straw rope used for ritual purification and ceremonies in Shinto. They can vary in diameter from a few centimeters to several meters, and are often festooned with paper streamers. *Shimenawa* indicate sacred or pure spaces, such as *torii* gates, and are often found at shrines and other sacred landmarks.

地主神 じぬしがみ

その土地の守護神。人が足を踏み入れる以前から、その地を占める神。「じしゅしん」ともいう。

注連縄 しめなわ

1本の縄に紙垂やわら束を下げたもの。神社の鳥居、社殿、手水舎など、とくに神聖性、清浄性を示す場所をあらわし、不浄な外界と区別する目印に用いる。

Chapter 2

Jinja Honcho

The administrative body of the Association of Shinto Shrines, it provides administrative support to roughly 80,000 shrines throughout Japan. Its grand shrine is Ise Jingu. *Jinja Honcho* promotes Shintoism and offers guidance to shrines and the training of Shinto priests.

Mizuhiki

Special strings made from tightly wound, starched paper in a variety of colors. It is used to create decorations and as a decorative tie wrapper for gifts, cards and envelopes such as *shugibukuro* (special gift money envelopes). *Miko* (shrine maidens) use it to tie back their long hair.

第二章

神社本庁
じんじゃほんちょう
全国の神社約8万社を包括する宗教法人で、本宗は伊勢神宮。神社神道の宣布をはじめ、包括する神社の指導、神職の養成などを行っている。

水引 みずひき
糊をひいて固めた紙紐。髪を束ねる元結に使用するほか、祝儀袋や進物用の包み紙を結ぶ時に用いる。

Chapter 3

Minamoto Yoritomo
(1147-1199)

The founder and first shogun of the Kamakura shogunate. As the head of the Minamoto warrior clan, descended from the imperial family, he raised the flag of revolt against the Taira clan which had dominated Japanese politics in Kyoto for years. After his victory in 1185, he established the shogunate, beginning a feudal age that lasted well into the 19th century.

Futaba Aoi

Asarum caulescens; a wild perennial plant that grows in all parts of Japan except Hokkaido and Okinawa. It is characterized by heart-shaped leaves that have historically been a popular decorative motif in Japan. Also appears in the family crest of the Tokugawa clan, who established the Edo shogunate in the early 17th century. In recent years, the plant has declined in abundance due to the damaging effects of both deer grazing and climate change, to an extent that Kyoto elementary schools have had to start cultivating it for use in the annual Aoi Matsuri festival.

第三章

源頼朝 みなもとのよりとも
(1147〜1199)
鎌倉幕府の初代将軍。源氏（天皇を祖先にもつ源姓の武家）のトップとして平氏と壮絶な戦いをして勝ち、東日本に初めて武家政権を樹立した。鎌倉幕府は1185年に実質的に成立したとされ、1333年に滅亡するまで約150年間続いた。

二葉葵 ふたばあおい
上賀茂神社・下鴨神社の神紋である二葉葵は、北海道・沖縄をのぞく日本各地に自生する野草。葵は、17世紀に武家政権を樹立した将軍徳川家の家紋（三葉葵）にも使われている。近年、鹿による食害、気象変動などで激減したため、京都の小学校でも二葉葵の栽培が始まり、葵祭に使用された。

Fujiwara Clan

A family of powerful regents descended from Nakatomi no Kamatari, an aide to Emperor Tenji in the 7th century, whose primary strategy to gain influence was to marry off their daughters to emperors. The Fujiwara dominated Japanese politics during the Heian period (794-1185) and had great influence over imperial decision-making and policy by monopolizing regent positions.

Tokugawa Ieyasu
(1542-1616)

The first shogun of the Edo shogunate. After his victory at the Battle of Sekigahara, he established the shogunate in Edo (presently Tokyo) in 1603 and ruled unchallenged until the end of his life. Thereafter, the Edo shogunate continued peacefully in power through fifteen shoguns for about 265 years, until the Meiji Restoration in 1868.

藤原氏 ふじわらし

7世紀に天智（てんじ）天皇の側近だった中臣鎌足（なかとみのかまたり）を祖とする貴族。鎌足の子、藤原不比等（ふじわらのふひと）が2人の娘を天皇の后（きさき）とし、初めて天皇家の外戚となった。2人の皇后は次代の天皇を生み、藤原氏は朝廷内の勢力を増し、12世紀まで王朝政権の中枢を占めた。

徳川家康
とくがわいえやす
（1542〜1616）

江戸幕府の初代将軍。日本を二分する関ヶ原の戦いで勝利し、1603年、江戸（現在の東京）に幕府を開いた。江戸幕府は以来、1867年に大政奉還するまで、15人の将軍によって265年続く。将軍と大名によって全国を統治し、内戦のない比較的平穏な日々が続いた。

Chapter 4

Sekihan

A festive dish of steamed rice with red beans. Although the combination of crimson (or red) and white has been regarded as auspicious since ancient times, the origin of this tradition is not certain. It is also explained that, durig festive times, *sekihan* is cooked because it resembles the customary auspicious dish of white mochi.

Ujigami

Guardian deities of a specific place. Originally these were *kami* of ancestor worship or of family ancestors. *Ubusunagami* is the *kami* of one's birthplace and *chinjugami* is the *kami* of an area, but those distinctions have disappeared today and they are generally known as *ujigami*.

Kazoedoshi

The traditional Japanese system of age reckoning. Newborns begin life at the age of one, with everyone gaining a year at New Year rather than on their birthdays. Thus, a child born in December would turn two less than a month after birth. Today, use of *kazoedoshi* is limited to traditional ceremonies, divinations, and obituaries.

第四章

赤飯 せきはん

紅(赤)と白の取り合わせは、古来めでたいものとされているが、その理由は定かでない。日本ではめでたい時に赤飯を炊き、白い餅を振る舞う習慣があるので、そこから来ているという説もある。

氏神 うじがみ

氏神はもともと、氏族の祖先神や、祖先が祀った氏族と関係の深い神のことをいった。また自分の祖先や自分の出生地を守護する神を産土神といい、一定地域の守護神を鎮守神といったが、今日ではそれらの区別がなくなり、いずれも氏神と呼ばれている。

数え年 かぞえどし

数え年は、生まれるとすぐ1歳と数えるもので、1月1日になるたびに1歳を加算していく。これに対し、現在、一般的に使われる満年齢は、生まれた時は0歳で、誕生日ごとに1歳を加算していく。

Yaku

A word associated with evil spirits and misfortune. *Yakudoshi* refers to certain years or ages in people's lives when they are especially prone to misfortune and bad luck. *Yakubi* are the specific days of misfortune when a person must be especially careful. *Yakubi* also simply means "an unlucky day."

Mikoshi

Portable Shinto shrines which are carried in procession on the shoulders of a group of carriers. They are exceptionally large, ornately decorated palanquins which can resemble miniature buildings. Shinto followers believe they serve as temporary vehicles to transport deities from one place to another during festivals, or during a move to a new shrine or other location.

厄 やく

わざわいや災難のこと。厄年のほかに、厄日もあり、この日は物事に対して慎重に振る舞わなければならないとされる。また、不愉快なことが多かった日を振り返って厄日という。

神輿 みこし

神霊が他所に移動する時に用いられる輿で、社殿の形をしたもの。神社の神霊を移し、祭礼の時などに担ぐ。8世紀ごろから神の乗り物として普及し、時代とともに輿に取りつける装飾も派手なものとなっていった。

Kagura

Literally "god entertainment," *kagura* refers to a specific type of sacred Shinto theatrical dance set to music.

It was originally a ceremonial art form tied closely to divination and the pacification of spirits, but has evolved over time and continues today as a vibrant part of living Shinto tradition and ritual. The dances are believed to have folkloric origins connected to the creation myths and can be seen today typically at festival time. *Kagura* incorporates sophisticated costumes, masks and choreography into its productions.

Yabusame

Japanese horseback archery in which mounted riders on a running horse shoot three arrows in succession at three wooden targets. It was performed by imperial guards in the 11th century and used as a method for samurai to hone their skills and remain battle-ready. *Yabusame* was introduced as a ritual dedicated to the *kami* at Tsurugaoka Hachimangu Shrine with encouragement from the Kamakura Shogunate in the late 12th century.

神楽 かぐら

祭りの時に、神をもてなすために奉納される歌舞音曲。宮中の官人たちが奉仕した神事歌謡系統の御神楽と、各地の民間で行われる神楽がある。

流鏑馬 やぶさめ

馬に乗りながら三つの的を次々に矢で射る武術。11世紀には宮中警護の武士によって行われており、12世紀末には鎌倉幕府の奨励もあって鶴岡八幡宮で行われるようになった。流鏑馬が神事として奉納されるようになったのもこのころである。

Sumo

The national sport of Japan; competitive full-contact wrestling, wherein a wrestler attempts to force another out of a circular ring or to touch the ground. *Sumo* was used as part of the Shinto religion and remains full of ritual elements, such as the use of salt for purification. Even today, some shrines have a *sumo* ring, or *dohyo*, in their precinct, and *yokozuna* (grand champion wrestlers) still perform a ceremonial entrance into the *dohyo* as a respectful tribute to the various *kami*. *Sumo* wrestling was originally a farming ceremony used as part of prayers for good harvests. It later became an event of the imperial court, and eventually evolved into today's Grand *Sumo*.

相撲 すもう

相撲は本来、力くらべに由来し、初めはレスリングのような格闘技で、豊作を祈る農耕神事の一環であった。その後、宮廷の行事として儀礼化し、さらに競技としての細かなルールが定まり、今日の大相撲となった。神社の奉納神事としても相撲や横綱の土俵入りが行われていて、土俵を常設している神社もある。

Spring *Matsuri* Festivals to Visit

February

2-4
Bean-Throwing Setsubun Festival
Yoshida Jinja,
Kyoto city, Kyoto

6
Oto Fire Festival
Kamikura Jinja,
Shingu city, Wakayama

1st Horse Day
Hatsu Uma Festival
Fushimi Inari Taisha,
Kyoto city, Kyoto

Early February
Sapporo Snow Festival
Sapporo city, Hokkaido

2nd Friday-Sunday
Namahage Folklore Mask Festival
Mayama Jinja,
Oga city, Akita

15-17
Yokote Snow Shelter Festival
Yokote city, Akita

17-20
Hachinohe Enburi Folklore Dance Festival
Hachinohe city, Aomori

March

1st Sunday-April 15
Sanno Sai Festival
Hiyoshi Taisha,
Otsu city, Shiga

ぜひ訪ねてみたい祭り【春】

● 2月2〜4日
節分祭　吉田神社　京都市

● 2月6日
お燈祭　神倉神社　和歌山県新宮市

● 2月初午の日
初午大祭　伏見稲荷大社　京都市

● 2月上旬
さっぽろ雪まつり　北海道札幌市

● 2月第2金曜〜日曜日
なまはげ柴灯まつり　真山神社　秋田県男鹿市

● 2月15〜17日
横手かまくら雪まつり　秋田県横手市

● 2月17〜20日
八戸えんぶり　青森県八戸市

● 3月第1日曜日〜4月15日
山王祭　日吉大社　滋賀県大津市

13

Kasuga Sai Ritual
Kasuga Taisha,
Nara city, Nara

April

7

**Aofushigaki
Sea Ritual**
Miho Jinja,
Matsue city, Shimane

10-11

**Itoigawa Kenka Fighting
Festival**
Amatsu Jinja,
Itoigawa city, Niigata

14-15

Spring Takayama Festival
Hie Jinja,
Takayama city, Gifu

2nd Sunday

Yasurai Festival
Imamiya Jinja,
Kyoto city, Kyoto

30-May 6

**Kurayami
Midnight Festival**
Okunitama Jinja,
Fuchu city, Tokyo

April-May in Tiger and Monkey Years

**Onbashira
Sacred Log Riding Festival**
Suwa Taisha, Suwa city, Chino city and
Shimosuwa town, Nagano

Spring begins in February according to the Japanese old calendar.

●3月13日
春日祭　春日大社　奈良市
●4月7日
青柴垣神事　美保神社　島根県松江市
●4月10〜11日
糸魚川けんか祭り　天津神社　新潟県糸魚川市
●4月14〜15日
春の高山祭　日枝神社　岐阜県高山市

●4月第2日曜日
やすらい祭　今宮神社　京都市
●4月30日〜5月6日
くらやみ祭　大國魂神社　東京都府中市
●4〜5月（寅・申年）
御柱祭　諏訪大社
長野県諏訪市・茅野市・下諏訪町

Summer *Matsuri* Festivals to Visit

May

1
Takaoka Mikurumayama Float Festival
Takaoka Sekino Jinja,
Takaoka city, Toyama

15
Kanda Matsuri Festival
Kanda Myojin,
Chiyoda ward, Tokyo

15
Aoi Matsuri Festival
Kamigamo Jinja, Shimogamo Jinja,
Kyoto city, Kyoto

3rd Friday-Sunday
Sanjya Matsuri Festival
Asakusa Jinja,
Taito ward, Tokyo

June

7-17
Sanno Matsuri Festival
Hie Jinja,
Chiyoda ward, Tokyo

2nd Saturday
Chagu Chagu Umakko Horse Festival
Takizawa city, Morioka city, Iwate

14
Otaue Shinji Rice Planting Ritual
Sumiyoshi Taisha,
Osaka city, Osaka

17 (old calendar)
Kangen Sai Court Music Festival
Itsukushima Jinja,
Hatsukaichi city, Hiroshima

ぜひ訪ねてみたい祭り【夏】

●5月1日
高岡御車山祭　高岡関野神社　富山県高岡市

●5月15日
神田祭例大祭　神田明神　東京都千代田区

●5月15日
葵祭　上賀茂神社・下鴨神社　京都市

●5月第3金曜～日曜日
三社祭　浅草神社　東京都台東区

●6月7～17日
山王祭　日枝神社　東京都千代田区

●6月第2土曜日
チャグチャグ馬コ　岩手県滝沢市・盛岡市

●6月14日
御田植神事　住吉大社　大阪市

●旧暦6月17日
管絃祭　厳島神社　広島県廿日市市

July

1-15
Hakata Gion Yamakasa Float Festival
Kushida Jinja,
Fukuoka city, Fukuoka

1-31
Gion Matsuri Festival
Yasaka Jinja,
Kyoto city, Kyoto

14
Nachi Fire Festival
Kumano Nachi Taisha,
Nachi Katsuura town, Wakayama

Last Saturday-Monday
Soma Wild Horse Chase
Minami Soma city and Soma city,
Fukushima

24-25
Tenjin Matsuri Festival
Osaka Tenmangu,
Osaka city, Osaka

28
Onda Rice Planting Festival
Aso Jinja,
Aso city, Kumamoto

4th Saturday-Sunday
Tenno Riverside Festival
Tsushima Jinja,
Tsushima city, Aichi

Summer begins in May according to the Japanese old calendar.

●7月1〜15日
博多祇園山笠　櫛田神社　福岡市

●7月1〜31日
祇園祭　八坂神社　京都市

●7月14日
那智の火祭り　熊野那智大社
和歌山県那智勝浦町

●7月最終土曜〜月曜日
相馬野馬追　福島県相馬市・南相馬市

●7月24〜25日
天神祭　大阪天満宮　大阪市

●7月28日
おんだ祭　阿蘇神社　熊本県阿蘇市

●7月第4土曜〜日曜日
天王祭　津島神社　愛知県津島市

Fall *Matsuri* Festivals to Visit

August

1-7, 2-7
Hirosaki Neputa, Aomori Nebuta Float Festival
Hirosaki city and Aomori city, Aomori

3-6
Akita Kanto Lantern Pole Festival
Akita city, Akita

12-15
Awa Odori Dance Festival
Tokushima city, Tokushima

13-16
Gujo Odori Night Dance Festival
Hachiman town, Gujo city, Gifu

26-27
Chinka Sai Fire Festival
Kitaguchi Hongu Fuji Sengen Jinja, Fujiyoshida city, Yamanashi

1 (old calendar)
Oyama Mountain Ritual
Iwakiyama Jinja, Hirosaki city, Aomori

September

1-3
Owara Kaze no Bon Dance Festival
Yatsuo town, Toyama city, Toyama

2-15
Tsuruga Matsuri Festival
Kehi Jingu, Tsuruga city, Fukui

ぜひ訪ねてみたい祭り【秋】

- ●8月1〜7日 弘前ねぷたまつり
- ●8月2〜7日 青森ねぶたまつり
  青森県弘前市・青森市
- ●8月3〜6日
  秋田竿燈まつり 秋田市
- ●8月12〜15日
  阿波おどり 徳島市
- ●8月13〜16日
  郡上おどり盂蘭盆会 岐阜県郡上市八幡町
- ●8月26〜27日
  鎮火祭(吉田の火祭り)
  北口本宮冨士浅間神社 山梨県富士吉田市
- ●旧暦8月1日
  お山参詣 岩木山神社 青森県弘前市
- ●9月1〜3日
  おわら風の盆 富山市八尾町
- ●9月2〜15日
  敦賀まつり 氣比神宮 福井県敦賀市

14-16
Tsurugaoka Hachimangu Reitaisai Festival
Tsurugaoka Hachimangu, Kamakura city, Kanagawa

Respect for the Aged Day
Kishiwada Danjiri Matsuri Festival
Kishiwada city, Osaka

15
Iwashimizu Sai Ritual
Iwashimizu Hachimangu, Yawata city, Kyoto

October

7-9
Nagasaki Kunchi Float Festival
Suwa Jinja, Nagasaki city, Nagasaki

9-10
Fall Takayama Festival
Sakurayama Hachimangu, Takayama city, Gifu

14-15
Nada Kenka Fighting Festival
Matsubara Hachiman Jinja, Himeji city, Hyogo

22
Kurama Fire Festival
Yuki Jinja, Kyoto city, Kyoto

Fall begins in August according to the Japanese old calendar.

●9月14〜16日
鶴岡八幡宮例大祭　鶴岡八幡宮
神奈川県鎌倉市
●9月敬老の日ごろ
岸和田だんじり祭　大阪府岸和田市
●9月15日
石清水祭　石清水八幡宮　京都府八幡市
●10月7〜9日
長崎くんち　諏訪神社　長崎市

●10月9〜10日
秋の高山祭　櫻山八幡宮　岐阜県高山市
●10月14〜15日
灘のけんか祭り　松原八幡神社
兵庫県姫路市
●10月22日
鞍馬の火祭　由岐神社　京都市

Winter *Matsuri* Festivals to Visit

October

11-17 (old calendar)
Kamiari Sai Ritual
Izumo Oyashiro,
Izumo city, Shimane

November

1st, 2nd and 3rd
Rooster Day

Tori no Ichi Festival
Otori Jinja

The Monkey - Horse Days
(old calendar)

Tanadhui Sea Ritual
Taketomi Island, Taketomi town,
Okinawa

2-4

Karatsu Kunchi Float Festival
Karatsu city, Saga

November-February
Takachiho Yokagura Night Ritual
Takachiho town, Miyazaki

December

3

Chichibu Yomatsuri Night Festival
Chichibu Jinja,
Chichibu city, Saitama

3

Morotabune Sea Ritual
Miho Jinja,
Matsue city, Shimane

10

Daito Sai Festival
Hikawa Jinja,
Saitama city

ぜひ訪ねてみたい祭り【冬】

●旧暦10月11〜17日
神在祭　出雲大社　島根県出雲市
●11月酉の日
西の市　全国各地
●11月上旬ごろ（旧暦甲申〜甲午の日）
種子取祭(タナドゥイ)　沖縄県竹富町
●11月2〜4日
唐津くんち　唐津神社　佐賀県唐津市

●11月中旬〜2月上旬
高千穂夜神楽　宮崎県高千穂町
●12月3日
秩父夜祭　秩父神社　埼玉県秩父市
●12月3日
諸手船神事　美保神社　島根県松江市
●12月10日
大湯祭　氷川神社　さいたま市

15-16 **Akiha Fire Festival** Akiha Jinja, Hamamatsu city, Shizuoka	2 **Dainichido Bugaku Dance Ritual** Ohirumemuchi Jinja, Kazuno city, Akita
15-18 **Kasuga Wakamiya Onmatsuri Festival** Kasuga Taisha, Nara city, Nara	3 **Tama Seseri Sacred Ball Scrambling Festival** Hakozakigu, Fukuoka city, Fukuoka
31-January 1 **Syourei Sai Ritual** Dewa Sanzan Jinja, Tsuruoka city, Yamagata	9-11 **Toka Ebisu Festival** Imamiya Ebisu Jinja, Osaka city, Osaka

January

1

Wokera New Year's Eve Festival
Yasaka Jinja,
Kyoto city, Kyoto

Winter begins in November according to the Japanese old calendar.

●12月15～16日
秋葉の火まつり　秋葉神社　静岡県浜松市
●12月15～18日
春日若宮おん祭　春日大社　奈良市
●12月31日～1月1日
松例祭　出羽三山神社　山形県鶴岡市
●1月1日
白朮祭　八坂神社　京都市

●1月2日
大日堂舞楽　大日霊貴神社
秋田県鹿角市
●1月3日
玉せせり　筥崎宮　福岡市
●1月9～11日
十日戎　今宮戎神社　大阪市

加藤健司 かとう けんじ

鶴岡八幡宮教学研究所所長。國學院大学講師。さまざまなレクチャーシップやリサーチスタディーなど、国際文化交流を通じ神道を世界に伝える。韓国諸大学、国際交流基金などでの日本文化教育経験を踏まえ、外国人観光客の多い鎌倉で、外国語ガイド研修や留学生講座などの国際化を推進。近著に『流鏑馬』日本語版・英語版（霞会館）、共著に『神道の美術』（平凡社）など。

岩﨑 隼 いわさき じゅん

マンガから水彩・油彩まで幅広く手がけるイラストレーター。実家は北海道小樽市の浄土真宗（三門徒派）専名寺。

英文監修
Christopher Cooling

英文翻訳
柳田崇道（鶴岡八幡宮教学研究所共同研究員）

編集協力
(株)日本アート・センター

項目執筆
山口直大

写真
芳賀ライブラリー／木村敬司

装丁・本文デザイン
金田一亜弥　高畠なつみ（金田一デザイン）

Bilingual Guide to Japan
SHINTO SHRINES
Second Edition

神社バイリンガルガイド 改訂版

2019年12月15日　初版　第1刷発行
2025年 8月13日　　　　第3刷発行

著　者	加藤健司　岩﨑　隼
発行者	高橋木綿子
発行所	株式会社小学館
	〒101-8001
	東京都千代田区一ツ橋2-3-1
	編集　03-3230-5118
	販売　03-5281-3555
印刷所	株式会社DNP出版プロダクツ
製本所	株式会社若林製本工場
DTP	株式会社昭和ブライト
編　集	矢野文子（小学館）

造本には十分注意しておりますが、印刷、製本など製造上の不備がございましたら「制作局コールセンター」（フリーダイヤル0120-336-340）にご連絡ください。（電話受付は、土・日・祝休日を除く9：30〜17：30）
本書の無断での複写（コピー）、上演、放送等の二次利用、翻案等は、著作権法上の例外を除き禁じられています。本書の電子データ化などの無断複製は著作権法上の例外を除き禁じられています。代行業者等の第三者による本書の電子的複製も認められておりません。

©2019 KATO Kenji／IWASAKI Jun
Printed in Japan
ISBN978-4-09-388745-8